Quick & Easy
Way To Learn French

Vishakha Sharma

QUALIS BOOKS

G T BOOK AGENCY

All rights reserved

This book, or parts thereof, may not be reproduced in any form without written permission of the publisher.

ISBN : 81-87838-02-7

1st Published 2005
13th Reprint 2022
Quick & Easy Way to Learn French

Published by
Qualis Books
E-219, New Rajinder Nagar
IInd Floor, New Delhi - 110060
qualisbooks@yahoo.co.in

Printed in India at
D.K. Fine Art Press (P) Ltd.
Delhi- 110052

Quick & Easy Way to Learn French

Before the emergence of English as the language of the masses, French was the lingua franca, of the cities all over Europe. Even in England, it was customary for the elite to learn to write and read in French. Over a period of time the English language overshadowed French, but for the foreign language lovers, it still remains one of the most sophisticated and intriguing language. A large number of people show a keen interest in learning this language.

Therefore, through the present book 'Quick & Easy Way to Learn French' an attempt has been made to introduce the French language.

The primary aim of the book is to teach those enthusiasts who have little or no acquaintance with the language. It contains all the essential nuances of the French grammar.

Key Note

Titles of the chapters are given in English so that the learners can easily understand the topic to be studied.

All letters, words and sentences are first given in English for the early understanding of the learner.

The pronunciation is given next to the French words and sentences.

CONTENTS

Part-I   **1-20**

Chapter 1 : Sounds of Alphabet and Vowels
Chapter 2 : The French Alphabet
Chapter 3 : Nasal Sounds
Chapter 4 : Consonants
Chapter 5 : How to Pronounce?

Part-II   **21-26**

Chapter 1 : Words of Two-Letters
Chapter 2 : Words of Three-Letters
Chapter 3 : Words of Four-Letters
Chapter 4 : Groups of Two Words
Chapter 5 : Groups of Three Words

Part-III   **27-29**

Chapter 1 . Salutations and Greetings
Chapter 2 : Basic Phrases

Part-IV   **30-79**

Chapter 1 : The Human Body
Chapter 2 : Animals, Birds, Water Animals, Insects
Chapter 3 : Breakfast, Lunch, Food & Drink, Vegetables, Fruits, Trees, Flowers
Chapter 4 : House, Cleaning Products, Dresses, Clothing, Beauty Shop, School, Family, Weights & Measures
Chapter 5 : Days of the Week, Months of the Year, Numbers, Attention, Seasons, Directions, Colours, Time, Time of the Day, Dates
Chapter 6 : Health & Ailments, Entertainment & Music, Fun & Games, Occupations, Professions, Business Contacts
Chapter 7 : Nations
Chapter 8 : Nature, Gems, Minerals

Part-V   **80-81**

Chapter 1 : Model Letter

Part-VI		82-83
Chapter 1	: Proverbs	

Part-VII		84-99
Chapter 1	: How to Ask the Questions	
Chapter 2	: How to Answer Questions	
Chapter 3	: Communicating	
Chapter 4	: Small Talk	
Chapter 5	: Socialising	
Chapter 6	: Going Out in the Evening	
Chapter 7	: What Do You Think?	
Chapter 8	: Basic Phrases	
Chapter 9	: Complaints	

Part-VIII		100-115
Chapter 1	: Asking the Way	
Chapter 2	: At the Reception	
Chapter 3	: At the Hotel	
Chapter 4	: At the Restaurant	
Chapter 5	: Lunch/Dinner	
Chapter 6	: Bank, Currency Exchange	
Chapter 7	: At the Post Office	
Chapter 8	: Telegrams, Telephone	
Chapter 9	: Going Shopping	

Part-IX		116-185
Chapter 1	: Basic French Grammar Rules, Tools, At the Bus Stop, On Bus, At the Station, Porter, On the Platform, Customs Control, In the Street, At the Airport, Bus, Taxi, Sightseeing & Excursions, Flowers, Book Shop, Vocabulary, Dry Goods, Fabrics, Toiletries, At the Beauty Shop, At the Barber Shop, At the Doctor's Clinic, On the Phone, Reading & Writing, Holidays, Date, Weather, Police: Lost & Found, Abbreviations, Signs	

In this chapter we shall study the sounds of alphabet and vowels.

(i) Vowels: Voyelle: Voyēl

While learning French we should be very careful in pronouncing vowels. All French vowels are pure vowels.

[ä] as 'a' in father

English	French	Pronunciation
Dad	papa	päpä
Banana	banane	banän
Sofa	sofa	sōfä
Pineapple	ananas	anänä
Turnip	navet	nävē
Boat	bateau	bäto
Bazaar	bazar	bazär
One Fourth/a quarter	quart	kür
Ship	navire	nävir
Advocate	avocat	ävokä
Ring	bague	bäg
Small note book	carnet	kärnē

(ii) Vowels:-

[e] as 'u' in butter.
[ē] as 'a' in ate.
[ê] as 'e' in met.
'e' is also a silent letter at the end of a word.

English	French	Pronunciation
Baby	bébé	bēbē
School	école	ēkol
Coffee	café	käfē
Number	numéro	nymēro
Mother	mère	mer
Anger	colère	ko
Feast	fête	fet
Model	modèle	model
Slide	glisser	glisē
Blade	lame	läm
Ill	malade	maläd
Axis	axe	äks
Sorrow, pain	peine	pēn
Hen	poule	pul
Buttock	fesse	fēs
Earth	terre	tēr
Laugh	rire	rir
Street	rue	ryu
Chicken	poulet	poulē
Rupee	roupie	rupi
Nine	neuf	nef
Actor	acteur	äkter

(iii) [i] as 'ee' in see.

English	French	Pronunciation
Friend	ami	ämi
Roast	rôti	roti
Pile	pile	pil
Bed	lit	li
Island	île	il
Rice	riz	ri
Radish	radis	rädi
Noon	midi	midi
Cabin	cabine	kabin
Laugh	rire	rir

(iv) [Ō] as 'O' in lot.
   [O] as 'O' in obey.

English	French	Pronunciation
Shoulder	épaule	ēpol
Calf	veau	vo
Sausage	saucisse	sosis
Jump	sautez	sotē
Sparrow	moineau	mwäno
Cake	gâteau	gäto
Boat	bateau	bäto

(v) [U] as 'U' in put.
    [U̱] as 'U' in burn.
    [o̅o̅] as 'oo' in cuckoo.

English	French	Pronunciation
Cuckoo	coucou	kuko̅o̅
Zulu	zoulou	zulu
Soft	mou	mu

(vi) 'eu' is pronounced as 'u' in butter

English	French	Pronunciation
Wish	voeu	ve
Thursday	jeudi	s̄edi
Egg	oeuf	ef
Old	vieux	viye
Europe	Europe	erop

Chapter 2

The French Alphabet, L'alphabet français, L'alphabē froñsē:-

English	Pronunciation
A	ä
B	bē
C	sē
D	dē
E	e
F	ēf
G	s̄ē
H	äz̄
I	i
J	s̄i
K	kä
L	ēl
M	ēm
N	ēn
O	o
P	pē
Q	kui
R	ēr
S	ēs
T	tē
U	yui
V	vē
W	dōōbl vē
X	iks
Y	igrek
Z	zed

Chapter 3

Nasal Sounds

Nasal Sounds have no equivalent sound in English.

(i) an is pronounced through nose:-

English	French	Pronunciation
When	quand	kan̄
Tall	grand	gran̄
Aunt	tante	tän̄t
Tent	tente	ten̄t
Bench	banc	ban̄
Time	temps	tom
Child	enfant	an̄fan̄

(ii) on̄ – o is pronounced through nose:-

English	French	Pronunciation
No	non	non̄
Bottom	fond	fon̄
Lemon	citron	sitron̄
Nylon	nylon	nilon̄
Lesson	leçon	leson̄
Lion	lion	liyon̄

(iii) en̄ – e is pronounced through nose.

English	French	Pronunciation
Full	plein	plen̄
Five	cinq	sen̄k
Simple	simple	semple
Train	train	tren̄
Sailor	marin	maren̄
Tomorrow	demain	demen̄

(iv) un̄ – u is pronounced through nose.

English	French	Pronunciation
Monday	lundi	lēndi
Brown	Brun	bren̄
Perfume	parfum	pärfum̄
Anyone	aucun	okun

Chapter 4

Consonants: Consonnes: koṉson

The following consonants when in combination of vowels has a different sound. So while learning French we should know the pronunciation of these consonants.

(i) <u>b is pronounced as 'be' in better.</u>

English	French	Pronunciation
Baby	bébé	bēbē
Reel	bobine	bōbin
Ring	bague	bäg
Beast	bête	bēt

(ii) <u>C is pronounced as 'k' in combination with a,o,u.</u>

English	French	Pronunciation
Coffee	café	käf ē
Camel	camille	kämi
Columbia	colombie	kolombi

(iii) <u>C is pronounced as 's' in combination with e,i,y.</u>

English	French	Pronunciation
Cycle	cycle	sikl
Cinema	cinéma	sinēma

English	French	Pronunciation
Sky	ciel	syl
Salt	sel	sēl
Cecil	cécil	sesil

(iv) When 'g' combines with a,o,u it has a hard sound as in.

English	French	Pronunciation
Gas	gaz	gäz
Boy	garçon	gärsoṉ
Garage	garage	gäräs̄
Gorge	gorge	gōrs̄
Rubber	gomme	gōm
Guitar	guitare	gitär
Counter	guichet	gichē

(v) J is pronounced as a sound in pleasure.

English	French	Pronunciation
Yellow	jaune	zhon
Jasmine	jasmin	zhäsmēṉ
Garden	jardin	zhärdēn
Toy	jouet	zhouē

(vi) L as in English.

English	French	Pronunciation
Wash	levez	levē
Leave	laissez	lēsē
Wool	laine	lēn

| Wing | aile | äyl |
| Ugly | laide | lēd |

(vii) M as in English.

English	French	Pronunciation
Ill	malade	maläd
Soft	mou	mōō
Ground	moulu	mulu
Telegram	télégram	tēlēgräm
Mother	mère	mēr

(viii) N as in English.

English	French	Pronunciation
Night	nuit	nuyi
Name	nom	noṅ
Turnip	navet	nävē
Snow	neige	nēzh
Nut	noix	nwa

(xi) P is pronounced as 'pe' in petrol.

English	French	Pronunciation
Bread	pain	peṅ
Rabbit	lapin	läpeṅ
Poison	poison	pwäzoṅ
Fish	poisson	pwäsoṅ
Petroleum	pétrole	petrōl

(x) R as in English.

English	French	Pronunciation
Round	rond	ro$\overline{n}$d
Row	rangée	ra$\overline{ns}$ $\overline{e}$
Near	près	pr$\overline{e}$
Very	très	tr$\overline{e}$
Laugh	rire	rir
Clear	clair	kl$\overline{e}$r

(xi) S as in English.

English	French	Pronunciation
Week	semaine	sem$\overline{e}$n
Mouse	souris	suri
Salt-box	salière	săliyer
Seat	siège	siye$\overline{s}$
Severe	sévère	s$\overline{e}$ver

(xii) T is pronouced as

English	French	Pronunciation
Toilet	toilette	twăl$\overline{e}$t
Cough	toux	tu
Tube	tube	tyub
Carpet	tapis	täpi
Deputy	député	d$\overline{e}$put$\overline{e}$

(xiii) V is pronouced as 'V' in van.

English	French	Pronunciation
Vain	vain	ven̄
Wine	vin	ven̄
Guest	invité	en̄vie̅
Old	vieux	vie
Poultry	Volaille	voleyi

Chapter 5

How to Pronounce?

The pronunciation of a French word is indicated in this book using a simplified system of phonetic notation. This notation is a simplified version of the International Phonetic System, which is mainly used by linguists. Our aim in doing so is that everyone should be able to use this book.

The 'key to pronunciation' presents the way how the French sounds are symbolised and their corresponding IPS (International Phonetic System) symbols. Whenever the learner finds it difficult to follow the pronunciation in any part of the book he is requested to consult then and there the 'key to pronunciation'.

Pronunciation: Prononciation: Prononsiyasiyon

The main difference between French and English pronunciation are as follows:
(i) English pronunciation has energetic stress and weak articulation of unstressed syllables.
(ii) In French every syllable has a clear and distinct sound.
(iii) In English syllables are sometimes slurred.
(iv) In French most syllables end with a vowel. In English many syllables end in consonants.

(v) In French final consonants are usually silent but in English final consonants are usually sounded.

(vi) French has weak-stress and energetic articulation of all syllables.

(vii) In French the final consonant of a word is usually linked to the initial vowel of the next if the words belong to the same grammatical group.

(viii) In French, before a word beginning with a vowel and mute 'h', the final 'e' or 'a' of monosyllable is dropped and placed by an apostrophe.

Key to Pronunciation

(i) **Guide de prononciation**
Gid de pronoṅsiyasiyoṅ

International phonetic symbol	As Enligh sounds	System followed in this Book
i	ee in see	i
e	a in ate	e
e	e in met	ē
a	a in father	a
a	aa in bazaar	ä
o	o in obey	o
o	o in lot	ō
u	u in put	u
y	ui	ui

e	silent letter at the end of the word.	
o	nasal sound in song	o$\overline{n}$
e	nasal sound in main	e$\overline{n}$
w	w in wet	w
h	h in hedge	h
b	b in bus	b
d	dh in dhal	d
f	f in fuse	f
g	g in go	g
z	sound in pl<u>ea</u>sure	$\overline{s}$
k	k in keen	k
l	l in lark, but not in full	l
m	m in man	m
n	n in nab	n
p	p in pot	p
r	r in rat	r
s	s in sun	s
v	v in van	v
x	sh in ship	$\overline{z}$
z	z in zip	z

Pronunciation Exercises

(ii) Exercises de prononciation
Exsersis de prononsiyasiyoṉ

Syllables

ba	be	bi	bo	bu	bé	bè	bê
ba	be	bi	bo	bu	be	b$\bar{e}$	b$\bar{e}$
ca	ce	ci	co	cu	cé	cè	
ka	se	si	ko	ku	se	s$\bar{e}$	
da	de	di	do	du	dé	dè	dê
dä	de	di	do	du	de	d$\bar{e}$	d$\bar{e}$
fa	fe	fi	fo	fu	fé	fè	fê
fä	fe	fi	fo	fu	fe	f$\bar{e}$	f$\bar{e}$
ga	gue	gui	go	gu	gué	guè	guê
gä	ge	gi	go	gu	ge	g$\bar{e}$	g$\bar{e}$
ja	je	jo	ju	jé			
zhä	zhe	zho	zhu	zh$\bar{e}$			
ka	ke	ki	ko	ku	ké		
kä	ke	ki	ko	ku	k$\bar{e}$		
la	le	li	lo	lu	lé	lè	lê
lä	le	li	lo	lu	le	l$\bar{e}$	l$\bar{e}$

ma	me	mi	mo	mu	mé	mè	mê
mä	me	mi	mo	mu	me	m$\bar{e}$	m$\bar{e}$
na	ne	ni	no	nu	né	nè	nê
nä	ne	ni	no	nu	ne	n$\bar{e}$	n$\bar{e}$
pa	pe	pi	po	pu	pé	pè	pê
pä	pe	pi	po	pu	pe	p$\bar{e}$	p$\bar{e}$
que	qui	qué	què	quê			
ke	ki	ke	k$\bar{e}$	k$\bar{e}$			
ra	re	ri	ro	ru	ré	rè	rê
rä	re	ri	ro	ru	re	r$\bar{e}$	r$\bar{e}$
sa	se	si	so	su	sé	sè	
sä	se	si	so	su	se	se	
ta	te	ti	to	tu	té	tè	tê
tä	te	ti	to	tu	te	t$\bar{e}$	t$\bar{e}$
va	ve	vi	vo	vu	vé	vè	vê
vä	ve	vi	vo	vu	ve	v$\bar{e}$	v$\bar{e}$
wa	we	wi	wo	wu			
wä	we	wi	wo	wu			
za	ze	zi	zo	zu	zé	zè	
zä	ze	zi	zo	zu	z$\bar{e}$	z$\bar{e}$	

[Note: $\bar{s}$ – sound as like that of pleasure]

Specific Pronunciation

(iii) Prononciation specifique
pronoñsiyasiyoñ spesifik

In French language different combinations of letters have specific pronunciation. Some of them are given below:-

		Sound 'e' (é, ez, er, et)
be	–	bé, bez, ber
de	–	dé, dez, der
sē	–	sé, cé, sez, cez, ser, cer

Note: $\bar{z}$ like English in she or machine, but not as ch in charles.

		Sound '$\bar{e}$' (è, ê, ai, ei, est, et, endings)
tē	–	tè, tê, téi, tai
rē	–	rè, rê, rai, rei, ret
gē	–	guè, guê, gai, guet
mē	–	mè, mê, mai, mei, met

		Sound ' eñ' (in, ein, ain, yn,)
beñ	–	bin
greñ	–	grin, grain
treñ	–	trin, train
señ	–	sin, sain, cein

Sound 'añ' (an, en)

klañ	–	clan, clen
kañ	–	can, kan, quan, quen
fañ	–	fan, fen, phan
rañ	–	ran, ren
sañ	–	sun, sen, Çan

Sound 'O' (O, an, eau)

ko	–	cau
rozo	–	roseau
mo	–	meau, mau
do	–	dau, dô, deau
to	–	tau, tcau

Sound 'oñ' (on)

soñ	–	son, çon
koñ	–	con, qu' ón
noñ	–	non, nom

Sound 'f' (f, ph)

fa	–	fa, pha
fo	–	fo, pho
fē	–	fé, phé

Sound 'k' (c, q, qu, k)

ka	–	ca, ka
ke	–	què, ke

Sound 's' (s, ç, ss, c)

sa	–	sa, ça
se	–	sé, cé
si	–	si, ci

Sound 'u' (ou)

tu	–	tou
su	–	sou
mu	–	mou

Sound 'wa' (oi)

twa	–	toi
rwa	–	roi
pwa	–	poi

Part-II
Chapter 1

Words of Two Letters

Les mots de deux lettres:-
lē mo dē de lē tr:-

English	French	Pronunciation
Some	du	dyu
And	et	ē
Here	ici	isi
Born	né	nē
Bare	nu	nyu
Gold	or	or
Bone	os	os
Or	ou	ōō
Where	où	ōō

Chapter 2
Words of Three Letters

Les mots de trois lettres:-
l̄e mo de trwä l̄e tr

English	French	Pronunciation
Age	âge	äs̄
Garlic	ail	ēl
Friend	ami	ämi
Ass	âne	än
Ball	balle	bäl
Low	bas	bä
Wheat	blé	blē
Key	clé	klē
Dowry	dot	do
Hard	dur	dur
Water	l'eau	lo
Fire	feu	fe
Gas	gaz	gäs̄
Island	île	il
Juice	jus	s̄yu
Lake	lac	läk
Bed	lit	li
Ache bad	mal	mäl
Sea	mer	mēr
Little	peu	pe

Rice	riz	ri
Street	rue	ryu
Salt	sel	sel
Soil	sol	sol
Summer	été	ētē
South	sud	syud

Chapter 3

Words of Four Letters

Les mots de quatre lettres:-
lē mo de kätr letr:-

English	French	Pronunciation
Help	aide	ed
Wing	aile	ēl
Car	auto	oto
Bath	bain	beñ
Bench	banc	bañk
Beast	bête	bēt
Well	bien	biyañ
Wood	bois	bwa
Coffee	café	käfē
Sky	ciel	sil
Nail	clou	klu
Hunger	faim	feñ

Liver	foie	fwä
Station	gare	gär
People	gens	s̄en̄
Pretty	joli	s̄oli
Milk	lait	lē
Read	lire	li:r
Moon	lune	lyun
Honey	miel	myēl
Price	prix	pris
Egg	oeuf	ef
Dream	rêve	rev
Cough	toux	tu

Chapter 4

Groups of Two Words

Groupes de deux mots
Grup de de mo

English	French	Pronunciation
I know	je sais	s̄e sē
I think	je crois	s̄e krwä
I understand	je comprends	s̄e kompron̄
Tell me	dites-moi	dit muwä
Give me	donnez-moi	donē muwä
Bring me	apportez-moi	aportē muwä

English	French	Pronunciation
Come to breakfast	venez dèjeuner	venē dēsenē
Good bye	au revoir	o revwä
Be punctual	soyez exacte	soyē exakt
Help yourself	servez vous	servē vōō
Not much	pas beaucoup	pa boku
Gather them	cueillez-les	kuyē lē
It rains/It is raining	il pleut	il pleu
Without fail	sans faute	sañ fot
Pretty well	assez bien	assē biyañ
Very little	très peu	tre peu
Very well	très bien	tre biyañ
With pleasure	avec plaisir	avek plēzir
Five minutes	cinq minutes	sēnk minyt

Chapter 5

Groups of Three Words

Groupes de trois mots:-
Grup de trwa mo:-

English	French	Pronunciation
At the latest	au plus tard	o pluy tärd
Unknown to me	à mon insu	ä moñ ēnsy
As for me	quant à moi	kañt ä muwä
You have a reason	vous avez raison	vuzävē rēzon

English	French	Pronunciation
Speak louder	parlez plus fort	parlē pluy hō
We have arrived	nous voilà arrivés	nu vwalä arivē
Give your ticket	remettez votre billet	remētē votr biyē
Hold my arm	tenez mon bras	Tenē moñ bra
Call the conductor	appelez le conductcur	apēlē le condyukter
I always loose	je perds toûjours	že pērd tuzhur
He always coughs	il tousse toujours	iltōōs tuzhur
I have cold	je suis enrhume	že swi eñrym
I am ill	je suis malade	že swi maläd
Come with me	venez avec moi	venē avek muwä
She is excellent	elle est excellente	ēlē texseleñt
Light the fire	allumez le feu	aluymē le fō
The last quarter	le dernier quartier	le derniyē kartiyē
It is dark	il fait sombre	Il fē sombr
I know him	je le connais	že le konē
In the fields	dans la compagne	dañ la kompän
She is well	elle est bien	el ē biyañ
Not at all	point du tout	pwañ duy tu
That is enough	cela est assez	sēla ē täsē
I must go	il faut partir	il fo partir
I thank you	je vous remercie	že vōō remērsi

Part-III
Chapter 1

SALUTATIONS AND GREETINGS

English	French	Pronunciation
Good-morning	bonjour!	boñzhōōr!
Good-afternoon	bonjour!	boñzhōōr!
Good-evening	bonsoir!	boñswar!
Good-night	bonne nuit!	boñuyi
Hello	salut!	sälyu
Hello	allô	älo
Welcome/Glad to see you	soyez le bienvenu	soyē le biyañ venu
Good-bye	au revoir!	ō revwä!
See you soon!	à bientôt!	ä biyañto!

Chapter 2

BASIC PHRASES

Les Phrases basique:-
Lē frāz basik:-

English	French	Pronunciation
Yes	oui	wi
No	non	nōn
Thank you	merci	mērsi
Thank you very much	merci beaucoup	mērsi boku
Thank you too!	merci à vous aussi!	mērsi ä vu zosi!
I (we) Thank you so much	je vous remercie!	s̄e vu remērsi
Enter!	entrez!	entrē!
Leave!	sortez	sortē!
If you please	s'il vous plait	sil vōo plē
Pardon	pardon!	pardoñ
No, thanks	non, merci!	nō mērsi
Thanks a million	mille merci	mi mērsi
Mention not	de rien	de riyañ
Certainly	certainement	sertēnmoñ
Of course	cela va sans dire	selä vä sañs dir
I would be glad to	très volontiers	trē volontiyēr
Good	bien!	biyañ!
Right!	c'est ça!	sē sä!
Terrific	super!	super
With pleasure!	avec plaisir!	avek ples̄ir

Never	jamais	s̄ ämē
Nothing	rien	riyan̄
Certainly not! (No way)	en aucun cas!	en̄ oken̄ kä
Out of question	pas question!	pa-kestiyon̄
Perhaps/May be	peut être!	petētr
Probably	probablement	probabelmon̄
All the best!	bonne chance!	bōn ʒäns
Have a good trip	bon voyage	bon̄ vōyäs̄
Please help me!	aidez-moi s'il vous plaît	aidē muwä sil vōō plē
Excuse-me	excusez-moi	exquzē-muwä
I am sorry	je suis désolé	ʒe swi desolē
	pardonnez-moi!	pärdonē-muwä
I am extremely sorry	je regrete infiniment	ʒe regrēt enfiniman
Please don't be angry	ne m'en veuillez pas	ne men veiē pä

Part-IV
Chapter 1

THE HUMAN BODY

LE CORPS:-
Le korps:-

English	French	Pronunciation
Face	visage	visās̄
head	tête	tēt
forehead	front	froñ
Eyes	yeux	iye
Ear	oreille	oreiy
Nose	nez	nē
Throat	earyngologiste	earynzhlozhist
Chin	menton	meñtoñ
Beard	barbe	barb
Mouth	bouche	bōoz
Lips	lèvres	lēvr
Tooth	dent	deñt
Neck	cou	ku
Shoulder	épaule	ēpol
Arm	bras	brä
Hand	main	mēn
Finger	doigt	dwät
Nail	ongle	oñgle

Chest	poitrine	pwätrin
Knee	genou	s̄enu
Leg	jambe	s̄amb
Foot	pied	piyēd
Abdomen	ventre	vontr
Ankle	cheville	shevil
Appendix	appendice	äpondis
Back	dos	dō
Bladder	vessie	vēsi
Bone	os	os
Collar Bone	clavicule	kläviqul
Invertibral-	invertébral-	envērtebräl-
disk	disque	disk
Gall bladder	bile	bil
Heart	coeur	ser
Hip	hanche	hänsh
Intestine	intestin	entēstin
Joint	articulation	ärtikulasiyon̄
Kidney	rein	ren̄
Liver	foie	fuwä
Lungs	poumons	pōomon̄
Muscle	muscle	musle
Nerve	nerf	nerf
Penis	pénis	pēni
Rib	côte	kot
Sinus	sinus frontal	sinus frōntäl
Skin	peau	pō
Spine	colone vertébral	kolon vertēbräl
Stomach	estomac	ēstomäk

Temple	temple	tēmpl
Thigh	cuisse	kwiss
Throat	gorge	gors̄
Toe	orteil	ortēl
Tongue	langue	lauñg
Vertebra	vertebra	vertēbrä

Chapter 2

ANIMALS

LES ANIMAUX:-
Lē zänimo:-

English	French	Pronunciation
Ox	boeuf	bef
Cow	vache	väz̄
Buffalo	buffle	boōfle
Bull	taureau	tōrō
Horse	cheval	shēväl
Mare	jument	zhumē
Dog	chien	shiyañ
Cat	chat	shä
Hare	lièvre	liēvr
Wild sheep	mouflon	mufloñ
Lion	lion	liyoñ
Tiger	tigre	tigr
Panther	panthère	pañther

English	French	Pronunciation
Bear	ours	urs
Gorilla	gorille	goriy
Chimpanze	chimpanzé	shimpänzhē
Fox	renard	renär
Jackal	chacal	shäkāl
Wolf	loup	lōop
Camel	chameau	shämō
Deer	daim	dēm
Zebra	zèbre	zēbr
Kangaroo	kangourou	kañgurōō

BIRDS

LES OISEAUX:-
Lezoazo:-

English	French	Pronunciation
Cock	coq	kok
Hen	poule	pul
Chicken	poulet	pulē
Duck	canard	kanärd
Goose	oie	owä
Pigeon	pigeon	pizhoñ
Dove	colombe	kolomb
Peacock	paon	pōn
Vulture	vautour	votōōr
Kite	milan	milän
Sparrow	moineau	mwäno
Nightingale	rossignol	rosinōl

English	French	Pronunciation
Parrot	perroquet	pērokē
Eagle	aigle	ēgle
Cuckoo	coucou	kukōō
Crane	grue	grōō
Crow	corbeau	korbo
Woodpecker	pic	pik
Black-Bird	merle	mērl
King Fisher	martin-pêcheur	marteñ pēsher
Whistling Bird	siffleur	sifler

WATER ANIMALS

LES ANIMAUX DE L'EAU:-
Lē zanimo de lo:-

English	French	Pronunciation
Frog	grenouille	grenueiye
Fish	poisson	pwäsoñ
Whale	baleine	bälēn
Crab	crabe	cräb
Eel	anguille	añgiye
Carp	carpe	kärp
Salmon	saumon	somoñ
Serpent	serpent	sērpeñ
Shark	requin	rekyiñ
Dolphin	dauphin	dofeñ

INSECTS

INSECTES:-
Ēnsekt:-

English	French	Pronunciation
Bee	abeille	äbiy
Butterfly	papillon	päpiyoṉ
Ant	fourmi	foōrmi
Fly	mouche	moōz̄
Grasshopper	sauterelle	soterēl
Spider	araignée	ärēnē
Mosquito	moustique	moōstik
Bug	punaise	punaiz

Chapter 3

Food Stuff, Vegetables, Fruits, Flowers

THE MEALS:-
LES REPAS:-
Lē rēpa:-

THE BREAKFAST

LE PETIT DEJEUNER:-
Le peti dēzhonē:-

English	French	Pronunciation
Bread	pain	peñ
Butter	beurre	ber
Eggs	oeufs	e
Milk	lait	lē
Tea	thé	tē
Coffee	café	käfē
Black Coffee	café noir	käfē nuwär
Honey	miel	mil
Orange Juice	jus d'orange	sus d'oränzh
Tomato Juice	jus de tomate	sus de tomēto
Toast	toast	tost
Jam	confiture	koñfityur
Cereal	céréale	sērēyäl

THE LUNCH

DEJEUNER:-
dezhōnē:-

English	French	Pronunciation
Beef	boeuf	bef
Meat	viande	viyänd
Mutton	mouton	mutoñ
Oil	huile	huyil
Rice	riz	ri
Salad	salade	saläd
Soup	soupe	sōōp
Ham	jambon	zhämboñ
Dish with/ of macroni	plat de macaronis	plä de mäkaroni
Noodles	nouille	nōōiyē

FOOD AND DRINK

Would you pass me...the please?
Vous pourriez / tu pourrais me passer..., s´il vous plaît / s´il te plaît?
vu puriyē / tu purē me päsē...sil vōō plē / sil te plē

Do you mind if I smoke?
Ça vous / te dèrange si je fume?
sa vōō / te dēranzh si zhe fume

Thank you for inviting me/us.
Merci pour l'invitation?
mērsi pōōr lenvitasiyoñ

It was wonderful.
C'était excellent.
sētē excelañ.

FOOD

NOURRITURE:-
Nooritiyur:-

English	French	Pronunciation
Alcohol	l'alcool	Lalkol
Appetizer	l'appéritif	läpēritif
Artificial sweetner	saccharine	säkrin
Ashtray	cendrier	sendriē
Available	libre	libr
Bar	bistrot	bistro
Beer	bière	biyēr
Bottle	bouteille	boteyi
Bread	pain	pēn
Bread roll	petit pain	petit pēn
White bread	pain blanc	pēn blank
Break fast	petit déjeuner	petit dēsenē
To bring	apporter	äportē
Butter	beurre	ber
Cake	gateau	gäto
Carafe	carafe	karäfe
Chair	chaise	chēz
Cheese	fromage	fromäs̄
Cocoa	cacao	käko

Coffee	café	käkäo
Black coffee	café noir	käfē nuwar
Coffee with milk	café au lait	käfē au lē
Cold	froid	frwäd
Cream	chantilly	ž̄antiyi
Crisp bread	pain croustillant	pēn krustiyän
Cup	tasse	täs
Desert	dessert	dēsēr
Diabetic (person)	diabetique	diabētik
Diabetic (special food)	diabetique	diabētik
Diet	régime	rēzhim
Dinner	dîner	dinē
Dish	plat	plä
Drink	boisson	bwäsoñ
To drink	boire	bwär
Drinks menu	carte des boissons	Kärt dē bwasoñ
To eat	manger	manzhe
Egg	l'oeuf	lef
Fried egg	l'oeuf au plat	lefoplä
Hard boiled egg	l'oeuf dur	lef dyur
Scrambled	l'oeuf brouillé	lef bruiyē
Soft boiled egg	l'oeuf a la coque	luf ä lä kok
Excellent	Excellent	exceleñ
Fat	gras	grä
Fatty	gras	grä
Fish	poisson	pwason
Fork	fourchette	fooržet
Knife	couteau	kuto
Fresh	frais/fraîche	frē / frēz

40 / Quick & Easy Way to Learn French

Fresh raw vegetable	crudites	krudit
Fruits	fruits	fruwi
To be full	ne plus avoir faim	ne pluzavwar fem̄
Garlic	ail	aiye
Glass	verre	vēr
Grease	gras	grä
Greasy	gras	grä
Ham	jambon	s̄ämbon̄
Hamburger	hamburger	hamburger
Hard	dur	dyur
To take breakfast	prendre le petit-déjeuner	prendr le petit-dēs̄enē

THE VEGETABLES

LES LEGUMES:-
Le legume:-

English	**French**	**Pronunciation**
Cucumber	concombre	kon̄ kombr
Pumpkin	citrouille	sitrueiy
Melon	melon	melon̄
Tarmarind	tamarind	Tämärin
Turnip	navet	nävē
Bean	haricot	häriko
Pea	pois	pwä
Radish	radis	rädi
Cabbage	choux	z̄oo

Carrot	betterave	betēräv
Asparagus	asperge	äspers̄
Carrot	carottes	kärōt
Mushroom	champignons	shampēnyōn
Cauliflower	chou-fleur	zōo fler
Spinach	épinards	ēpinär
Onion	oignons	owänōn
Potatoes	pommes de terre	pom de tēr
French fries	frites	fri
Tomato	tomates	tomät

THE FRUITS

LES FRUITS:-
Lē fruit

English	French	Pronunciation
Banana	banane	banän
Orange	orange	oräns̄
Apple	pomme	pom̄
Peach	pèche	pez̄
Plum	prune	prun̄
Strawberry	fraise	frēz
Cherry	cerise	seriz
Pineapple	ananas	anänä
Mango	mangue	manḡ
Apricot	apricot	äpriko
Almonds	amandes	ämōnd
Peanuts	cacahouètes	käkähuēt

English	French	Pronunciation
Lemon	citron	sitron̄
Coconut	coco	koko
Dates	dattes	dät
Figs	figues	fig
Raspberries	framboises	främbwäz
Chestnut	marron	maro͞on
Nuts	noix	nwä
Pear	poire	pwär
Grapes	raisins	rēzin

THE TREES

LES ARBRES:-
Lezarbr:-

English	French	Pronunciation
Apple Tree	pommier	pomiyēr
Cashewnut	acajou	akäzhu
Pine	pin	pin
Oak tree	chêne	shēn
Pear	poire	pwär
Palm tree	palmier	pälmiyē
Walnut tree	noyer	noyē
Coco	koko	koko
Tamarind	tamarin	tämärin̄

THE FLOWERS

LES FLEURS:-
Lē flur:-

English	French	Pronunciation
Bouquet	bouquet	bukē
Rose	rose	roz
Lily	lis	li
Tulip	tulipe	tulip
Violet	violette	violēt
Lotus	lotus	lotus
Jasmine	jasmin	s̄äsmeñ

Chapter 4

House and its Parts, Domestic Articles, Weights and Measure Coins, Dress, Make-up

THE HOUSE

LA MAISON:-
La Mezōn:-

English	French	Pronunciation
Hall	salle	säl
Dining hall	salle à manger	säl ä mansē
Room	chambre	shambr
Bedroom	chambre à coucher	shambr ä kushē
Kitchen	cuisine	quizin
Garden	jardin	zhärdēn
Roof	toit	twät
Wall	mur	myur
Bell	sonnette	sonēt
Apartment	appartement	äpärtmeñ
Balcony	balcon	bälkoñ
Bathroom	salle de bains	säl de baiñ
Bathtub	baignoire	bēnwär
Bed	lit	li
Linen	draps	dräp
Side lamp	lampe de chovat	lamp de shovä
Blanket	couverture en laine	kōōvertēr en lēn
Broom	balai	bälē

Cabin	cabane	käbän
Chair	chaise	chēz
Table	table	täbl
Closet	placard	plakärd
Cold water	l'eau froide	lo frwäd
Cup	tasse	täs

CLEANING PRODUCTS

Les produits de nettoyage:-
Lē produi de netoyäzh:-

English	French	Pronunciation
Dirty	sale	säl
Dishes	vaisselle	vēsēl
Door	porte	port
Door lock	serrure	sēryur
Drinking water	l'eau potable	lo pōtäble
Electricity	électricité	ēlēktrisitē
Elevator	l'ascenseur	äsenser
Floor	étage	ētäs̄
Flush	chasse d'eau	shäs do
Gas cylinder	bouteille de butane	bōōtei de bētän
Glass	verre	ver
Hot water	eau chaude	ō chod
Key	clé	klē
Lamp	lampe	lamp
Light bulb	ampoule	ämpōōl
Luggage	bagages	bägäzh

English	French	Pronunciation
Maid	femme de chambre	fam de zambr
Mattress	matelas	mātēla
Pillow	oreiller	oreiyē
Plate	assiette	äsiyēt
Plug	fiche	fish
Pool	piscine	pisin
Refrigerator	réfrigérateur	rēfrizherätur
Shower	douche	dōōsh
Sink (bathroom)	lavabo	levābo
Sink (Kitchen)	évier	ēviyē
Stairs	éscalier	eskaliyē
Telephone	téléphone	tēlēfon
Toilet	toilette	twälēt
Towel	serviette	sērviyēte
Trash	ordures	ordyur
Window	fenêtre	fenētr

THE DRESSES

LES HABITS:-
Lē zhäbi:-

English	French	Pronunciation
Coat	manteau	monto
Waistcoat	gilet	zhilē
Pant	culotte	kulot
Trouser	pantalon	päntälon̄
Gloves	gants	gan̄

English	French	Pronunciation
Boots	bottes	bot
Shirt	chemise	shēmiz
Handkerchief	mouchoir	mushwär
Belt	cienture	siyäntur
Skirt	jupe	zhup
Top	blouson	bluzoñ
Dress	robe	rob
Socks	chausettes	shosēt
Shoes	chaussures	shosur
Stocking	bas	bä

CLOTHING

LES VÊTEMENTES:-
Lē vētmen:-

English	French	Pronunciation
Apron	tablier	täbliyē
Bathing cap	bonnet de bain	bonēt de bēn
Bathing suit/trunk	maillot de bain	mäyo de bēn
Bathrobe	peignoir	peñwär
Belt	cienture	siyäntur
Bikni	bikini	bikni
Blouse	chemisier	shemiziyē
Blue jeans	bleu-jeans	blu s̄iñ
Bra-brassière	soutien-gorge	sōōtiēn-gorzh
Cap	casquette	käsket
Cardigan	veste	vēst

Coat	manteau	monto
Corset	corset	kōrsē
Dress	robe	rob
Dressing gown	robe de chambre	rob de shombr
Gloves	gants	gan
Handkerchief	mouchoir	mōōshwär
Jacket (lady's)	veste	vest
Jacket (man's)	veston	veston̄
Socks	chausettes	shosēt
Leather coat	manteau de cuir	monto de kwir
Leather Jacket	blouson en cuir	bluzon en kwir
Lingerie	lingerie	lenzheri
Nightie	chemise de nuit	chēmiz de nwi
Pajamas	pyjama	pizhämä
Panties	slip	slip
Pants/Trouser	pantalon	pantälon̄
Pants suit	costume	kostum
Parka	anorak	änoräk
Petticoat	jupon	zhupon̄
Rain coat	imperméable	ēmpermebl
Scarf	écharpe	ēsharp
Shirt	chemise	shēmiz
Shorts	short	short
Skirt	jupe	s̄up
Slip	jupon	s̄upon̄
Sportswear	vêtements de sport	vētmen de sport
Stockings	bas	bä
Stole	étole	ētol
Suit (lady's)	tailleur	taiyer

Suit (man's)	costume	kostum
Tie	cravate	krävät
Underpants	caleçon	kälsoñ

THE BARBER/BEAUTY SHOP

LE MAGASIN DE BEAUTÉ:-
Le magäzen de butē

English	French	Pronunciation
Barber	coiffeur	kwäfer
Beard	barbe	bärb
Beauty parlour	salon de beauté	sälon de butē
Comb (noun)	peigne	pēnye
Comb (verb)	peigner	penye
Curls	boucles	bookl
Cut	couper	kōōpe
Dandruff	pellicules	pēlikul
Do S.O.S. hair	coiffer	kwäfer
Dye	teindre	tēndr
Hair	cheveaux	shevo
Hair cut	coup de cheveaux	kup de shevo
Dry hair	secs	sek
Greasy hair	gras	grä
Hairdo	coiffeur	kwäter
Hairdresser	coiffeur	kwäfer
Hair-drier	séchoir	sēshwär
Hair-loss	chute des cheveaux	shyut dē zevo
Manicure	manicure	maniqur

Moustache	moustaches	mōōstäz̄
Pedicure	pédicure	pēdiqur
Scalp massage	massage de la tête	mesās̄ de lä tēt
Set	mettre en plis	mettre enpli
Shave	faire la barbe	fēr lä barb
Side burns	favoris	fävori
Strand	mèche	mēz̄
Wash	laver	lävē
Wig	perruque	pēruk

THE SCHOOL

ÉCOLE:-
ēkol:-

English	French	Pronunciation
Classroom	salle de classe	säl de clas
Matron	maître	mētr
Teacher	instituteur	ēnstituter
Professor	professeur	profēsur
Student	élève	elev
Black-board	tableau noir	täblo nwär
Note-book	carnet	kärnē
Note-book	cahier	kähiē
Book	livre	livr
Paper	papier	päpiyē
Pen	stylo	stilō
Pencil	crayon	kräyon̄

THE FAMILY

LA FAMILLE:-
La fami:-

English	French	Pronunciation
Aunt	tante	tänt
Boy	garçon	gärsoñ
Brother	frère	frēr
Sister	soeur	ser
Mother	mère	mēr
Father	père	pēr
Brother-in-law	beau-frère	bō-frēr
Cousin (female)	cousine	kōōzin
Cousin (male)	cousin	kōōzen
Daughter	fille	fee
Daughter-in-law	belle-fille	bēl-fee
Father-in-law	beau-père	bō-pēr
Grand-child	petit-fils	petit-fis
Grand-daughter	petite-fille	petit-fee
Grand-father	grand-père	groñ-pēr
Grand-mother	grand-mère	groñ-mēr
Grand-parents	grands-parents	groñ-pärēn
Husband	mari	märi
Mother-in-law	belle-mère	bēl-mēr
Nephew	neveau	nevo
Niece	nièce	nies
Parents	parents	pähoñ

Sister-in-law	belle-soeur	bēl-ser
Son	fils	fis
Son-in-law	gendre	s̄endr
Wife	femme	fam

WEIGHTS AND MEASURES

English	**French**	**Pronunciation**
1 Milimeter	un milimètre	en melimētr
1 Centimeter	un centimètre	en sentimētr
1 Decimeter	un décimètre	en dēsimētr
1 Meter	un mètre	en mētr
1 Kilometer	un kilomètre	en kilomētr
1 Inch	un pouce	en pus
1 Mile	une lieue	yun liyu
1 Nautical mile	un mille marin	en mil merēn
1 Square meter	un mètre carré	en mētr kärē
1 Litre	un litre	en litr
1 Pound	un demi kilo	en dēmi kilo
1 Ton	une tonne	yun tun
A piece (of...)	un morceau (de...)	en mōrso
A pair (of...)	une paire (de...)	yun pēr (de...)
A dozen	une douzaine	yun doozēn (de...)
A packet (of...)	un paquet (de...)	en pakē (de...)

Chapter 5

Days, Months, Numbers, Seasons, Directions, Colours, Time, Time of the Day, Dates.

THE DAYS OF THE WEEK

Les jours de la semaine:-
Lē s̄ur de la semain:-

English	French	Pronunciation
Monday	lundi	lēndi
Tuesday	mardi	märdi
Wednesday	mercredi	merkredi
Thursday	jeudi	zhedi
Friday	vendredi	veñdredi
Saturday	samedi	samdi
Sunday	dimanche	dimonz̄

THE MONTHS OF THE YEAR

Les mois de l'année:-
Lē muwa de lannee:-

English	French	Pronunciation
January	janvier	s̄enviyē
February	février	fēvriyē
March	mars	märs
April	avril	ävril
May	mai	mē
June	juin	s̄uen̄
July	juillet	s̄uiyē
August	août	ut.....
September	septembre	sēptōmbre
October	octobre	ōktobre
November	novembre	novōmbre
December	décembre	dēsōmbre

THE NUMBERS

Les Nombres:-
Lē nombr:-

English	French	Pronunciation
1 One	un	uñ
2 Two	deux	de
3 Three	trois	trwä
4 Four	quatre	kätr.
5 Five	cinq	señk
6 Six	six	sis
7 Seven	sept	sēt
8 Eight	huit	huit
9 Nine	neuf	nef
10 Ten	dix	dis
11 Eleven	onze	oñz
12 Twelve	douze	dōoz
13 Thirteen	treize	trēz
14 Fourteen	quatorze	kätorz
15 Fifteen	quinze	kēnz
16 Sixteen	seize	sēz
17 Seventeen	dix-sept	dissēt
18 Eighteen	dix-huit	dizuit
19 Nineteen	dix-neuf	disnef
20 Twenty	vingt	veñ
21 Twenty-one	vingt et un	veñtēun
22 Twenty-two	vingt-deux	veñtde

23	Twenty-three	vingt-trois	veṉt trwä
24	Twenty-four	vingt-quatre	veṉt kätr
25	Twenty-five	vingt-cinq	veṉt seṉk
26	Twenty-six	vingt-six	veṉt sis
27	Twenty-seven	vingt-sept	veṉt sēt
28	Twenty-eight	vingt-huit	veṉt wit
29	Twenty-nine	vingt-neuf	veṉt nef
30	Thirty	trente	trant
31	Thirty-one	trente et un	trantē uṉ
32	Thirty-two	trente-deux	trant de
33	Thirty-three	trente-trois	trant trwä
34	Thirty-four	trente-quatre	trant kätr
35	Thirty-five	trente-cinq	trant seṉk
36	Thirty-six	trente-six	trant sis
37	Thirty-seven	trente-sept	trant sēt
38	Thirty-eight	trente-huit	trant huit
39	Thirty-nine	trente-neuf	trant nef
40	Forty	quarante	kēhont
41	Forty-one	quarante et un	kēhontē eṉ
42	Forty-two	quarante-deux	kēhont - de
43	Forty-three	quarante-trois	kēhont - trwä
44	Forty-four	quarante-quatre	kēhont - kätr
45	Forty-five	quarante-cinq	kēhont - seṉk
46	Forty-six	quarante-six	kēhont - sis
47	Forty-seven	quarante-sept	kēhont sēpt
48	Forty-eight	quarante-huit	kēhont huit
49	Forty-nine	quarante-neuf	kēhont nef
50	Fifty	cinquante	seṉkont
51	Fifty-one	cinquante et un	seṉkont un

52	Fifty-two	cinquante-deux	señkont de
53	Fifty-three	cinquante-trois	señkont trwä
54	Fifty-four	cinquante-quatre	señkont kätr
55	Fifty-five	cinquante-cinq	señkont señk
56	Fifty-six	cinquante-six	señkont sis
57	Fifty-seven	cinquante-sept	señkont set
58	Fifty-eight	cinquante-huit	señkont wit
59	Fifty-nine	cinquante-neuf	señkont nef
60	Sixty	soixante	swasoñt
61	Sixty-one	soixante et un	swasoñtē un
62	Sixty-two	soixante-deux	swasoñt de
63	Sixty-three	soixante-trois	swasoñt trwä
64	Sixty-four	soixante-quatre	swasoñt kätr
65	Sixty-five	soixante-cinq	swasoñt señk
66	Sixty-six	soixante-six	swasoñt sis
67	Sixty- seven	soixante-sept	swasoñt sēt
68	Sixty-eight	soixante-huit	swasoñt huit
69	Sixty-nine	soixante-neuf	swasoñt nef
70	Seventy	soixante-dix.	swasoñt dis
71	Seventy-one	soixante et onze	swasoñt oñz
72	Seventy-two	soixante-douze	swasoñt dōōz
73	Seventy-three	soixante-treize	swasoñt trēz
74	Seventy-four	soixante-quatorze	swasoñt kētorz
75	Seventy-five	soixante-quinze	swasoñt keñz
76	Seventy-six	soixante-seize	swasoñt sēz
77	Seventy-seven	soixante-dix-sept	swasoñt dissēt
78	Seventy-eight	soixante-dix-huit	swasoñt dizwit
79	Seventy-nine	soixante-dix-neuf	swasoñt disnef
80	Eighty	quatre-vingts	kätr veñ

81	Eighty-one	quatre vingt-un	kätr veñ eñ
82	Eighty-two	quatre vingt-deux	kätr veñ de
83	Eighty-three	quatre vingt-trois	kätr veñ trwä
84	Eighty-four	quatre vingt-quatre	kätr veñ kätr
85	Eighty-five	quatre vingt-cinq	kätr veñ señk
86	Eighty-six	quatre vingt-six	kätr veñ sis
87	Eighty-seven	quatre vingt-sept	kätr veñ sēt
88	Eighty-eight	quatre vingt-huit	kätr veñ wit
89	Eighty-nine	quatre vingt-neuf	kätr veñ nef
90	Ninty	quatre vingt-dix	kätr veñ dis
91	Ninty-one	quatre vingt-onze	kätr veñ oñz
92	Ninty-two	quatre vingt-douze	kätr veñ dōōz
93	Ninty-three	quatre vingt-treize	kätr veñ trēz
94	Ninty-four	quatre vingt-quatorze	kätr veñ ketorz
95	Ninty-five	quatre vingt-quinze	kätr veñ kēnz
96	Ninty-six	quatre vingt-seize	kätr veñ sēz
97	Ninty-seven	quatre vingt-dix-sept	kätr veñ dissēt
98	Ninty-eight	quatre vingt-dix-huit	kätr veñ dizwit
99	Ninty-nine	quatre vingt-dix-neuf	kätr veñ disnef
100	Hundred	cent	señ
1000	Thousand	mille	mil
10000	Ten thousand	dix mille	di mil
100000	Hundred-thousand	cent-mille	señ-mil
	One million	un million	eñ milyoñ

ATTENTION

Attention:-
Atte̅nsiyon̅:-

(i) Count the 30's, 40's, 50's, 60's and 80's in the same way as 20-29.
(ii) For 70-79 add 10-19 to soixante (60) and for 90-99 add 10-19 to quatre-vingts (80).
(iii) Quatre vingts has an 's' in vingt but in quatre vingt un there is no 's'.

SEASONS

Saisons:-
s̅ezon̅:-

English	French	Pronunciation
Year	année	än̅e̅
Month	mois	muwä
Spring	printemps	pren̅tan̅
Summer	été	e̅te̅
Autumn	automne	otom
Winter	hiver	ive̅r

DIRECTIONS

Directions:-
Dirēksiyon̄:-

English	French	Pronunciation
North	nord	nor
South	sud	syud
East	est	ēst
West	ouest	uēst
North-west	nord-ouest	nordouēst
North-east	nord-est	nordēst
South-east	sud-est	syudēst
South-west	sud-ouest	syudouēst

COLOURS

Couleurs:-
kooler:-

English	French	Pronunciation
White	blanc	blon
Black	noir	nwär
Green	vert	vēr
Red	rouge	rus̄
Blue	bleu	ble
Grey	gris	gri

Yellow	jaune	zhoñ
Rose/pink	rose	roz
Orange	orange	oränzh
Violet	violet	viyolē
Brown	brun	brēn

TIME

Temps:-
temp̄:-

English	French	Pronunciation
Minute	minute	minute
Hour	heure	er
Quater of an hour	quart d' heure	kärtder
Half an hour	demi-heure	demi-er
Day	jour	s̄ur
Morning	matin	mäteñ
Noon	midi	midi
Afternoon	après-midi	äpremidi
Evening	soir	swär
Night	nuit	nuyi
Midnight	minuit	minuyi

THE TIME OF THE DAY

Le temps du jour:-
le tem̄p du zhur:-

English	French	Pronunciation
What time is it?	quelle heure est-il?	kēler ētil?
It is 1 o'clok	il est une heure	ilē uner
It is 2 o'clok	il est deux heures	ilē dezer
It is 3 o'clok	il est trois heures	ilē trwäzer
It is 4 o'clok	il est quatre heures	ilē kätrer
It is 5 o'clok	il est cinq heures	ilē sanker
It is 6 o'clok	il est six heures	ilē sizer
It is 7 o'clok	il est sept heures	ilē sēter
It is 8 o'clok	il est huit heures	ilē huiter
It is 9 o'clok	il est neuf heures	ilē nuver
It is 10 o'clok	il est dix heures	ilē dizer
It is 11 o'clok	il est onze heures	ilē onzer
It is noon/12 o'clock	il est midi	ilē midi
It is six hrs. 5 min.	il est six heures cinq	ilē sizer sēnk
It is quater past seven	il est sept heures quart	ilē sēter kärt
It is 8 hours and 30 minutes	il est huit heures et demie	ilē huiter demi
It is 9 hours less one quater	il est neuf heures moins le quart	ilē nuver muwa le kärt
Around eleven	vers onze heures	veroñzer
9:30 sharp	à neuf heures trente précises	ä nuver trant prēsiz

From 8 till 9 (o'clock)	de huit heures à neuf heures	de huiter ā nuver
Between 10 and 12	entre dix et douze	ēntr dizē dōōz
Not before 7 p.m.	pas avant dix-neuf heures	pä ävoñ dis nuver
Just after 9 o'clock	un peu après neuf heures	eñpē aprē nuver
In half an hour	dans une demi-heure	danzyun demiur
It's too late	il est trop tard	ilē tro tard
It is still too early	il est encore trop tôt	ilē enkor trō tō

DATES

Dates:-
dat:-

English	French	Pronunciation
Today	aujourd' hui	oṡordwi
Yesterday	hier	iyēr
Day before yesterday	avant-hier	ävantiyēr
Tomorrow	demain	demēn
Day after tomorrow	après-demain	apre demēn
Day before yesterday	veille	vēiy
Day after next day	lendemain	leñdemeñ
Week	semaine	sēmēn
Last week	semaine dernière	sēmēn derniyēr
Next week	semaine prochaine	sēmēn prochēn

A week ago/ eight days back	il y a huit jours	il yä wīsur
Within a week	dans la huitaine	dañ lä huyitēn
A fortnight ago	il ya quinze jours	il yä kēnz sur
Within a fortnight	dans la quinzaine	dañ lä keñzen
Last month	mois dernier	muwä derniyē
Next month	mois prochain	muwä procheñ
Last year	année dernière	änē derniyēr
Next year	année prochaine	änē procheñ

Chapter 6

**Health and Ailments, Entertainment and Music
(Concert Musical Instrument, Theatre and Music)**

HEALTH & AILMENTS

Maladie:-
Malädi

English	French	Pronunciation
AIDS	sida	sidä
Allergy	allergie	älersi
Appendicitis	appendicite	äpendisit
Asthma	asthme	äsm
Bite	morsure	morsyur
Bleeding	saignement	senyemen
Blister	ampoule	ämpoul
Blood	sang	san
Blood poisoning	empoisonnement du sang	ampwazonmen du san
Blood pressure	tension	tensiyon
High blood pressure	hypertension	hypertensiyon
Low blood pressure	hypotension	hypotensiyon
Blood transfusion	transfusion de sang	transfuziyon de san
Blood type	groupe sanguin	grup sänguen
Broken	cassé	käse
Bruise	contusion	kontuziyon

English	French	Pronunciation
Burn	brûlure	brulyur
Cardiac arrest	infarctus	infärktus
Plaster	plâtre	plätre
Doctor's certificate	certificat (mé dical)	sertifika (mē dikal)
Chicken pox	varicelle	värisel
Colic	colique	kolik
Concussion	commotion cérébrale	komosiyoñ serebräl
Conjunctivitis	conjonctivite	konsonktivitē
Constipation	constipation	konstipasiyoñ
Contagious	contagieux	kontäzhiye
Cough	toux	tōō
Cramp	cramp	krämp
Cystitis	systite	sistit
Dermatologist	dermatologue	dermätolog
Diabetes	diabète	dyabēt
Diarrhea	diarhée	dyarē
Dislocated	luxé	luxē
Dizziness	vertiges	vertis̄
Doctor (male)	médecin	mēdseñ
Doctor (female)	femme médecin	fēm medseñ
Ear infection	otite	otit
Doctor (ENT)- Ear, nose, throat	oto-rhino-laryngologiste	oto rino lärynsō-larynzholozhist
To faint	s'evanouir	sēvanuir
Fever	fièvre	fiyēvr
Flu	grippe	grip
Food poisoning	intoxication-alimentaire	intoxikasiyoñ-älimentēr

Fungal infection	mycose	mikoz
Gallstones	calcul billiare	kälkul biliyer
Measeles	rubéole	rubēol
Gynaecologist	gynécologue	s̄inokolog
Headache	mal de tête	mäl de tēt
Heart	coeur	ker
Heart attack	crise cardiaque	kriz kärdyäk
Hernia	hernie	hērny
Hospital	hôpital	hopitäl
Infection	infection	enfeksiyon̄
Inflammation	inflammation	enflamasiyon̄
Injury	blessure	blēsyur
Kidney stones	calcuis rénaux	kalkus rēno
Menstruation	menstruation	menstruasiyon̄
Migraine	migraine	migren̄
Mumps	oreillons	oreiyon̄
Nausea	nausées	nozē
Nosebleed	saignements-de nez	senmon̄-de nēz
Office Hours	heures de consultation	er de consultasiyon̄
To operate	opérer	operēr
Pain	douleurs	dolēr
Paediatrician	pédiatre	pēdyatr
Pneumonia	pneumonie	nimoni
To prescribe	prescrire	prēskrir
Pulled ligament	elongation	ēlongasiyon̄
Pulled muscle	claguage musculaire	klagäzh muskulēr
Pus	pus	pus

Shivering	frissons	frisoñ
Shock	choc	shok
Sore throat	mal de gorge	mäl de gōrs̄
Sprained	foulé	fo͞olē
Sting	piqûre	pikyur
Stomach-ache	mal à l'éstomac	mäl ä l'ēstomä
Stroke	attaque	atäk
Sunstroke	insolation	ensolēsiyoñ
Sunburn	coup de soleil	ko͞o de solei
Sweating	sueur	ser
Swelling	enflure	enflyur
Tetanus	tétanos	tētäno
Tick	tique	tik
Vaccination	vaccination	väksinäsiyoñ
Vaccination-record	carnet de-vaccination	karnē de-väksinäsiyoñ
Vomiting	vomissements	vomisemeñ
Ward	service	sērvis
To x-ray	faire une radio	fēr yun rädyo

ENTERTAINMENT AND MUSIC

Amusement et musique (concert/theatre et musique):-
ämyuzmen̄ e muzik (consert/theätr et muzik):-

English	French	Pronunciation
Piano	piano	pyäno
Pianist	pianiste	pyänist
Piano recital	récital de piano	rēsitäl de pyano
Piece of music	morceau de musique	morso de muzik
Play	pièce	pyes
Violin	violon	vyolon̄
Violin recital	récital de voilon	rēsital de vyolon̄
Music	musique	muzik
Musical	musical	muzikäl
Musician	musicien	muzisiyen̄
Opera	opéra	opēra
Orchestra	orchestre	orkēstr
Part/role	rôle	rol
Performance	représentation	reprēzentasiyon̄
Producer	producteur	produkter
Production	production	produksiyon̄
Programme	programme	prögräm
Scenery/settings	décor	dēkor
Stage	scène	sēn
Set designer	décorateur	dēkorätur
Singer	chanteur	shäntur
Singing	chant	shänt

English	French	Pronunciation
Song	chanson	zänsoñ
Soloist	soliste	zlist
Folk song	chanson populaire	zänson populēr
Song recital	récital de chant	rēsital de zāñ
Stage director	metteur en scène	mēter en sēn
Theatre	théâtre	theätr
Ticket	billet	biyē
Ticket sales	vent de billet	vēnt de biyē
Tragedy	tragédie	träsēdi
Comedy	comédie	kōmēdi
Work	oeuvre	evre
Accompanist	accompagnateur	äkompanyater
Act	acte	äkt
Actor	acteur	äkter
Actress	actrice	äktris
Applause	applaudissements	äplodismeñ
Ballet	ballet	bälē
Balcony	balcon	bälkoñ
Band	orchestre	orkēstr
Box office	caisse	kēs
Chorus	choeur	ker
Composer	compositeur	kompoziter
Concert	concert	konsēr
Concert hall	salle de concert	sal de konsēr
Conductor	chef d'orchestre	shēf d'orkēstr
Costumes	costumes	kostum
Costume designer	costumier	kostumiyē
Curtain	rideau	rido
Dancer	danseur	dänser

Director	metteur en scène	mētrensen
Drama	drame	dräm
Duet	duo	duo
Intermission	entracte	enträkt
Lobby	foyer	foyē

FUN AND GAMES

English	French	Pronunciation
Bar	bar	bär
Discotheque	discothèque	diskotēk
Ice skating rink	patinoire	pätinwär
Miniature golf course	minigolf	minigolf
Night club	une boîte de nuit	yun bwät de nuit
Tennis court	un court de tennis	en kōōr de tēnis
Play badminton	jouer au volant	šuer o voloñ
Play miniature-golf	jouer au mini-golf	šuer o mini-golf
Play ping-pong	jouer au ping-pong	šuer o ping-pong
Watch the fashion-show	aller voir-défilé de mode	alē vwar de-dēfilē de mod
Amusement	distraction	disträksiyoñ
Beauty contest	concours de beauté	konkōōr de butē
Card game	jeu de cartes	še de kärt
Circus	cirque	sirk
Club	club	kleb
Country fair	fête populaire	fēt populēr
Dice	dé	dē

Magazine	revue magazine	revu magazēn
Fashion magazine	journal de mode	sōornäl de mod
Newspaper	journal	sōornäl
Party games	jeux de société	se de sosiyētē
Pastime	passe-temps	pästoṁ
Radio	radio	rädiyo
Record player	électrophone	ēlektrofon
Tape recorder	magnétophone	magnētofoṅ
Television	télévision	tēlēvizyoṅ
News	informations	enformasiyoṅ

THE OCCUPATIONS

Les Occupations:-
le okupasiyon

English	French	Pronunciation
Craftsman	artisan	ärtizaṅ
Baker	boulanger	bulonzhē
Brewer	brasseur	bräser
Book-binder	relieur	rēlier
Barber	coiffeur	kwäfur
Carpenter	menuisier	menuziyē
Driver	chauffeur	shōfer
Pharmacist	pharmacien	farmasiyeṅ
Doctor	médecin	mēdseṅ
Grocer	épicier charcuterie	ēpisiē shärkuteri
Miller	menuier	menuier

Mason	maçon	mäsoñ
Smith	forgeron	forzherōn
Saddler	sellier	seliēr
Tailor	tailleur	taiyer
Shoe Maker	cardonier	kardoniyē
Teacher	instituteur	ēnstituter
Professor	professeur	profēser

THE PROFESSIONS

Les Professions:-
le profesyon

English	French	Pronunciation
Artist	artiste	ärtist
Auto mechanic	mécanicien	mēkänisiyañ
Bank teller	employé de banque	employē de bonk
Book keeper	comptable	komptäbl
Book seller	libraire	librēr
Brick layer	maçon	mäsoñ
Butcher	boucher	bushe
Carpenter	menuisier	mēnuzie
Chef	chef cusinier	shef quizinie
Civil servant	fonctionnaire	fonksiyonēr
Cobbler	cordonnier	kordoniyē
Computer programmer	programmeur	programer
Confectioner	pâtissier	pätisiyē
Cook	cuisinier	quiziniyē
Dentist	dentiste	dontist

Dress maker	tailleur	taiyen
Electrician	électricien	ēlēktrisyeñ
Farmer	agriculteur	ägrikultur
Fisherman	pêcheur	pēsher
Gardner	jardinier	s̄ärdiniyē
Lawyer	avocat	ävokä
Librarian	bibliothécaire	bibliyotēkēr
Notary	notoire	notwär
Optician	opticien	optisiyañ
Painter	peintre	piyañtr
Plumber	plombier	plombiyē
Pupil	élève	ēlev
Salesperson	vendeur	vonder
Scientist	scientifique	siyantifik
Sculptor	sculpteur	skulpter
Secretary	secrétaire	sēkrēter
Student	étudiant	etudiyañ
Teacher	instituteur/ professeur	enstituter/ profēser
Technician	technicien	tēknisiyañ
Trainee	apprenti	äpronti
Translator	traducteur	traducter
Truck driver	camionneur	kamiyoner
Veterinarian	vétérinaire	vēterinēr
Waiter	serveur	sērver
Waitress	serveuse	sērvuz
Watch maker	horloger	ōrlos̄ē
Writer	écrivain	ēkrivēn

BUSINESS CONTACTS

English	French	Pronunciation
Address	adresse	ädrēs
Appointment	rendez-vous	rōndē voo
Booth	stand	ständ
Brochures	documentation	dokumentäsiyoñ
Building	bâtiment	bätimeñ
To call on the- telephone	téléphoner	tēlēfonē
Catalogue	catalogue	kätalog
Convention	congrès	kongrē
Corporation	groupe industrial	grup endustrial
Conference	conférence	kōnférance
Conference room	salle de conférence	säl de kōnférance
Copy	photocopie	fotokopi
Client	client	klien
Department head	chef de service	shef de service
Documents	documents	dokumeñ
Earphones	casque	kask
Fax machine	téléfax	tēlēfäx
Hall (auditorium)	hall	hal
Information	information	enformasiyoñ
Interpreter	interprète	enterprēt
Management	direction	direksiyoñ
Manager	gérand	s̄ ērañ
To meet	Rencontrer	renkontrē
Meeting (discussion)	conférence	kōnfērens
Meeting (get together)	rencontre	renkoñtr

English	French	Pronunciation
News	message	mesāṡ
Office	bureau	byuro
Photocopier	photocopieur	fotokopiyer
Price	prix	pri
Price list	liste des prix	list dēpri
Prospectus	prospectus	prospektus
Reception	réception	rēcēpsiyoṅ
Representative	représentant	reprēzantant
Secretary	secrétaire	sēkretēr
Session	séance	sēans
Speech	exposé	ēkspozē
Telephone	téléphone	tēlēfon

Chapter 7

NATIONS

Nations:-
Nāsiyoṅ:-

English	French	Pronunciation
Germany	Allemagne	älemañye
Belgium	Belgique	bēlsik
Denmak	Danemark	dänmärk
England	Angleterre	änglētēr
France	France	Fräns
Holland	Hollande	holänd
Hungary	Hongrie	hongry
Ireland	Irelande	irländ

English	French	Pronunciation
Italy	Italie	itäli
Pakistan	Pakistan	päkistan
India	Inde	ēnd
Japan	Japon	s̄äpoñ
Mexican	Mexique	mēxik
Morocco	Maroc	moroko
Africa	Afrique	äfrik
Canada	Canada	cänädä
Brazil	Brésil	brēzil
Russia	Russie	rusi
Switzerland	Suisse	swis
Scotland	Ecosse	ēkos
Sweden	Suede	suēd
Spain	Espagne	ēspänye
America	Amérique	ämērik

Chapter 8

Nature, Gems, Minerals

NATURE

La nature:-
la näture:-

English	French	Pronunciation
God	dieu	diye
Air	air	ēr
Earth	terre	tēr

English	French	Pronunciation
Fire	feu	fe
Island	île	il
Lake	lac	läk
Moon	lune	lyun
Star	étoile	ētwäl
Sun	soleil	solēy
Sky	ciel	sil
River	rivière	riviyēr
World	monde	mond
Flower	fleur	fler
Tree	arbre	ärbr

GEMS

Gems:-
zhēm:-

English	French	Pronunciation
Ruby	rubis	ruybi
Coral	corail	korēl
Diamond	diamant	diyämen̄
Emerald	emeralde	emēräld
Lapis lazuli	lapis lazuli	lapi lazyli
Pearl	perle	perl
Saphire	saphir	säfir
Topaz	topaze	topäz

MINERALS

Minéraux:-
minēro:-

English	French	Pronunciation
Metals	métaux	mēto
Gold	or	or
Silver	argent	ärzhoṉ
Copper	cuivre	quivr
Aluminium	alluminium	älyminyum
Zinc	zinc	zink
Brass	cuivre jaune	quivr zhoṉ
Iron	fér	fēr
Steel	acier	äsiyē
Tin	étain	ēten

Part-V

MODEL LETTER

Lettre modèle:-
le̅tr mode̅l:-

10th August, 2004
Paris

My dear Rahul,

I am well. I hope you are also doing well. I am in Paris for the past two months. I have already visited some important towns in France. In Paris, the houses are very modern. The University of Paris — Sorbonne is very famous in the world. There are students from all the countries.

That is all for the time being. I shall write more in the next letter.

With love,

Your friend
Deepak

Le 10 août, 2004
Paris

Mon Chèr Rahul,
Je vais bien ici. Comment-allez vous? Je te souhaite une bonne santé. J'habite depuis deux moi à Paris. J'ai déjà vu quelques villes importantes de France. À Paris, les maisons sont très modernes. L'université de Paris — Sorbonne est très célèbre dans le monde. Il y a des étudiants de toutes nationalités.

C'est tout pour le moment. Je te donnerai d'autres nouvelles dans ma lettre prochaine.

Amicalement,

Ton ami
Deepak

Part-VI

THE PROVERBS

Health is better than wealth.
Qui n'a santé n'a rien.
ki nä säntē nä riyän̄.

A penny saved is a penny gained.
Il n'y a pas de petites économies
il ni yä pä de petit ēkonomi.

One must take the good and the bad together.
Qui épouse femme épouse les dettes.
ki ēpuz fem ēpuz lē dēt.

Pitchers have ears.
Les murs ont des oreilles.
lē mýur oñ dēzoreiy.

Love me little, love me long.
Qui aime bien, tard oublie.
ki ēm biyan̄, tärd ubliyē

Fortune comes when least expected.
Le bien vient en dormant.
le biyan̄ viyän̄ en̄ dormon̄.

Every mother's child is handsome.
La chouette trouve, ses petits beaux.
lä shouet truv sē petit bō.

A present given, brings one in return.
Qui chapon donne, chapon lui vient.
ki shäpoñ doñ, shapon luyi viyañ.

To know a thing thoroughly.
Savoir une chose sur le bout du doigt.
sävwär yun shoz suyr le bu duy dwä.

Christmas comes once a year.
Ce n'est pas tous les jours fête.
se nē pä tus lē s̄ur fēt.

Old friends are the best.
Vieux amis, vieux écus.
viyezämi viyēzēku.

A brave man does not need a long sword.
A vaillant homme courte épée.
Ä väyoñ om kōōrt ēpē.

Part-VII Chapter 1

HOW TO ASK THE QUESTIONS

Posez les questions:-
pozē lē kestiyoṅ:-

English	French	Pronunciation
Who?	qui? / qui est-ce?	ki / kiēs?
What?/Which?	quel?	kel?
Whose is it?	c'est à qui?	kēski?
Who is she?	qui est-ce?	kiēs?
What is this	qu'est-ce que c'est?	kēskesē?
Where?	où?	ōō?
How?	comment?	komoṅ
Why?	pourquoi?	purkwä
Is there?	y a-t-il?	yätil

Chapter 2

HOW TO ANSWER THE QUESTIONS

Comment répondre:-
komen repondr

1. Yes I understand.
   Oui, je comprends.
   wi, ṡe komproñ

2. No, I do not understand.
   Non je ne comprends pas.
   noñ ṡe ne komproñ pä.

3. There is no mistake.
   Il n' y a pas de faute.
   il niyä pä de fot.

4. It is good.
   C'est bien
   sē biyäñ

5. That is very bad.
   Ça c'est très mal.
   sä sē tre mäl

6. I congratulate you.
   Je vous félicite.
   ṡe voō fēlisit

7. You have done very well.
   Vous avez très bien réussi.
   vōō zävē tre biyän rēusi.

8. I will not allow you to do that.
   Je ne vous permet pas de faire cela.
   zhe ne vōō pērmē pä de fēr selä.

9. You have failed in your exam.
   Vous avez échoué à votre examen.
   vōō zävē eshuē ä votr exämen.

10. You have done well in your exam.
    Vous avez passé un bon examen.
    vōō zävē passē uñ boñ exämen

11. I wish he would come.
    Je voudrais qu'il vienne.
    zhe vudrē kil viyän.

12. He will see you tomorrow.
    Il vous verra demain.
    il vōō vērä demēn.

Chapter 3

COMMUNICATING

1. Does anyone here speak English?
   Il y a ici quelqu'un qui parle anglais?
   ilyä isi kelkan ki parl ēnglē?

2. Do you speak French?
   Vous parlez français?
   vōō parlē fransē?

3. Only a little.
   Un petit peu seulement.
   en petit pu sulmeñ.

4. Please speak a little slower.
   Parlez plus lentement, s'il vous plaît.
   parlē plōō lentmeñ sil vōō plē.

5. Do you understand?
   Vous compreney / tu comprends?
   vu komprenē / tu kompren?

6. Yes, I understand.
   oui, j' ai compris.
   wi s̄e kompri.

Chapter 4

SMALL TALK

Good morning, Sir/madam/miss.
Bonjour monsieur. / madame / mademoiselle
Boñzhur misyu / madäm / mademoizēl

How are you?
Comment – allez vous?
komoñtälē vu?

Very well.
Très bien.
tre biyäñ.

What is your name?
Comment vous appelez-vous / tu t'appelles?
komo vōō zäpēlē vōō / tu tāpēl?

My name is..................
Je m appelle....................
s̄e mäpēl........................

Where do you come from?
D'où venez vous / viens tu?
dōō venē vōō / viyañtu?

I come from......................
Je viens de......................
s̄e viyāñ de....................

Are you married?
Est-ce-que vous êtes / tu es marié?
esk vuzēt / tu ē märiye?

Yes, I am married / No, I am not Married.
Oui, je suis marié / Non je ne suis pas marié.
wi, ĕe swi märiyē / nō, ĕe ne swi pä märiyē.

Do you have children?
Est-ce-que vous avez / tu as des enfants?
ēsk vōō zävē / tu ä dēz enfeñ?

Do you have brothers or sisters?
Est-ce-que vous avez / tu as des frères et soeurs?
esk vōō zävē / tu ä dēfrēr ē sur?

Yes, I have a sister / a brother.
Oui j'ai une soeur / un frère.
wi, jhē yun ser / en frēr.

What is your age?
Quel âge avez-vous? / as-tu?
keläzh ävē vōō? / ä tu?

I am..........................years old.
J'ai............................ans.
zhē..........................añ.

What do you do?
Qu'est-ce-que vous faites?
kēsk vōō fēt?

I am a (an).....................
Je suis............................
zhe swi...........................

Is this your first time here?
C'est la première fois que vous venez / tu viens?
sē lä premyer fwa ke vōō venē / tu viyäñ?

Yes, this is the first time.
Oui, c'est la première fois.
wi sē lä premyer fwa.

No, I was in France..................time(s) before.
Non, c'est la................fois que je viens en France.
nō sē lä..................fwä k jhe viyän en Fräns.

How long have you been here?
Vous êtes / tu es là depuis combien de temps?
voo zēt / tu ē lä depui kombyan de tom?

Since....................days / weeks.
Dupuis.................jours / samaines.
depui....................zhoōr / semēn.

How much longer will you be staying here?
Vous restez / tu restes encore combien de femps ici?
voo rēstē / tu rēst enkor kombyän de temp isi?

I am leaving tomorrow.
Je pars demain.
ȷe pär demēn.

Another week / two weeks.
Encore une semaine / quinze jours.
onkor yun semēn / kēnz zhoōrs.

Do you like it here?
Ça vous / te plaît ici?
sä voō / te plē isi?

I like it very much.
Ça me plaît beaucoup.
sä me plē boku.

Chapter 5

SOCIALISING

What are you doing tomorrow?
Qu'est-ce-que vous faites / tu fais demain?
kēsk vōō fēt / tu fē demēn?

Shall we get together tomorrow / this evening?
Si oñ se voyait demain / ce soir?
si oñ se voyē demēn / se swär?

With pleasure.
Avec plaisir.
ävek pläzir.

It is not possible, since I already have plans.
Ce n'est pas possible. Je suis déjà pris / prise.
se nē pä posible. s̄e swi dēzhä pri / pris.

Would you like to join me for dinner this evening.
Si on dinait ensemble ce soir?
si oñ dinē ensembl se swär?

Yes, why not!
Oui, volontiers!
wi, volontiyē!

No, I am not free this evening. I am sorry.
Non, je ne suis pas libre ce soir. Je suis desolé.
nō, zhe ne swi pä libr se swär. s̄e swi dēsolē.

Chapter 6

GOING OUT IN THE EVENING

I would like to invite you to............................
Je voudrais vous inviter / t'inviter à......................
zhe vōō drē vu envitē / t'envitē ā..........................

Where shall we meet?
Nous nous voyons où?
nōō ensemblōn ōō

Let's meet at....................o'clock.
Disons qu'on se rencontre à.................heures.
dįzon koñ se renkoñtr ä.................er.

I will pick you up at...................o'clock.
Je passerai vous / te prendre à....................heures.
zhe päserai vōō / te prendr ä....................er.

Shall I see you again?
On se revoit?
on se rewä

Chapter 7

WHAT DO YOU THINK?

What do you think?
Qu'est-ce que vous pensey?
kēske vōō pensē

It was/is very nice here.
C'était / c'est très agréable ici.
sētē sē trezägrēble isi.

Great! / Very good.
Très bien!
trē biyän.

Wonderful!
Magnifique!
mänifik

Fantastic!
Formidable!
formidābl

I like that.
Ça me plaît.
sä me plē.

No, I did not understand.
Non, je n'ai pas compris.
nō zhe nē pä kompri.

Would you please repeat that?
Vous pourriez répéter, sil vous plaît?
vōō pōōriyē rēpētē sil vōō plē

What is this called in French?
Comment ça s'appelle en français?
komo sä säpēl en frensē

What does.................mean?
Que signifie....................?
ke signifi

With great pleasure.
Très volontiers.
tre volontiye.

O.K.
D'accord.
däkor.

It's all same to me.
Ça m'est égal.
sa metēgäl.

Whatever you like.
Comme vous vouley.
kom vōō vōōlē.

I do not know yet.
Je ne sais pas encore.
zhe ne sē pä zoṅkor.

May be.
Peut-être.
petētr.

Probably.
Probablement.
probäblemēn.

Too bad!
Dommage!
domäs̄!

Unfortunately, it is not possible.
Ce n'est malheureusement pas possible.
se nē malerzenmeṅ pä possibl.

I don't like that.
Ça ne me plaît pas.
sä ne me plē pä.

Absolutely not.
En aucun cas.
enoken kä.

No way!
Pas question!
pä kēstiyoñ!

No thanks.
Non, merci.
non mērci.

I already have plans.
J'ai déjà quelque chose de prévu.
ʒe dēsä kelke ʒoz de prēvyu

I am waiting for someone.
J'attends quelqu un.
zhäten kelkän.

Leave me alone.
Laissez - moi tranquille!
lēsē mwä trankil!

Get lost!
Casse - toi!
käs twä!

Chapter 8

BASIC PHRASES (PLEASE, THANK YOU)

Yes please.
Oui, volontiers.
wi voloṅtiyē.

No, thank you.
Non, merci.
nō mērsi.

That was very nice of you.
C'était très aimable de votre part.
sētē trezēmäbl de votr pär.

You are welcome.
Je vous en prie.
s̄e vōōzēn pri.

It does not matter.
Il n'y a pas de quoi.
il nyäpä de kvä.

May I?
Vous permettez?
vōō pērmētē?

I AM SORRY

Excuse me!
Excusez - moi! / Excuse - moi!
ēxcuzē mwä / ēxcuse mwä!

I am sorry.
Je suis désolé.
zhe swi dēsolē.

It was a misunderstanding.
C'était un malentendu.
sētēn mēläntēndu.

BEST WISHES

Congratulations!
Meilleurs veux!
mēyer ve!

Happy birthday!
Joyeux anniversaire! Bon anniversaire!
s̄oye äniv̄erser! boñ äniv̄erser!

Get well soon!
Bon rétablissement!
boñ r̄etäblismeñ

Good luck!
Bonne chance!
bōn z̄oñs!

Have a good trip!
Bon voyage!
boñ voyäs̄!

Have fun!
Amusez - vous bien!
ämuzē voo biyäñ!

Merry christmas!
Joyeux noël!
s̄oye noēl.

Happy new year!
Une bonne et heureuse année!
yun bōn ē erez änē!

Chapter 9

COMPLAINTS (HOTEL)

The shower / light does not work.
La douche / lumière ne marche pas.
lä dōosh / luminiyēr ne märz̄ pa.

The toilet does not flush.
La chasse d'eau ne marche pas.
lä shäs do ne märz̄ pa.

There is no hot water.
Il n'y a pas d'eau (chaude).
Iln'yä pä dō (z̄od)

The window does not open / close.
La fenêtre ne s'ouvre / ferme pas.
lä fenētr ne sōovre / fērm pä.

I can not lock the door to my room with key.
Ma porte ne ferme pas à clé.
mä port ne fērm pä ä klē.

The faucet drips.
Le robinet goutte.
le robinē gōot.

The drain is blocked.
L'écolement est boucheé.
lēkolmeñ ē bōoshē.

Could I please have another blanket?
Est-ce-que je pourrais avoir une couverture s'il vous plaît?
ēsk še purai avwär yun kuvērtyr sil vōo plē.

Could I please have some more dish please?
Est-ce-que je pourrais avoir des torchons s'ilvous plaît?
ēsk še purai avwär dē torshoñ sil vōo plē?

Could I have another towel please?
Est-ce-que je pourrai avoir une serviette s'ilvous plaît?
ēsk še purai avwär yun sērviēt sil vōo plē?

Could I have some clothes hanger please?
Est-ce-que je pourrai avoir quelques cintres s'ilvous plaît?
ēsk še purai avwär kēlk sintr sil vōo plē?

Part-VIII Chapter 1

ASKING THE WAY (ON THE ROAD)

Where is (are)...............?
Où est (sont).................?
ōō ē (soñ).....................

How do I get to..................?
Pour aller à..........................?
pōōr alē ä..........................

Is this the road to................?
Est-ce que c'est la route de................?
ēsk lä rōōt de........................

How many kilometers is it to the next town?
Combien de kilomètres y-a-t-il jusqu' à la prochain ville?
kombiyäñ de kilomētr yä til ṣuskä lä proshēn vil

Is this the right way to...............?
Est-ce la bonne direction pour.............?
ēs lä boñ direksiyoñ pōōr...............

How long?
Combien de temps?
kombyäñ de temp

How far is it to..............?
C'est loin d'ici (à)...............?
sē luwäñ disi (ä).............

Where (to)..............?
Où..............?
o͞o..............?

Would you please show me that on the map?
Indiquez-le moi sur la carte, silvous plaît?
endikē le muwa sur la kart sil vo͞o plē?

Where can I rent a car?
Je peux louer une voiture où?
zhe pe luwē yun vwätur o͞o?

......With chauffeur?
......arec chauffeur?
......avēk shofer?

For two (6) people.
Pour deux (six) personnes.
po͞or de (sis) pērson.

For one day (one week, two weeks).
Pour un jour (une semaine, deux semaines)
po͞or un s̄oor (yun semēn, de semēn)

How much will it cost?
Ça coûte combien?
sa ko͞ot kombiyan̄?

Will I have to pay for the gasoline myself?
Dois-je payer l'essence moi-même?
dwä-s̄e pēyē lēsense mwä-mēm?

How much do I have to deposit?
Je dois vous verser une caution de combien?
s̄e dwä vo͞o vērsē yun kausiyon de kombiyan̄?

When (where) can I pick up the car?
Quand (où) peux je venir chercher la voiture?
kon (o͞o) pui-s̄e venir z̄erz̄e lä vwätur

Fast.
Vite.
vit.

Slow.
Lentement.
lontmoñ.

Chapter 2

AT THE RECEPTION

Au Réception:-
O Rē sepsiyon̄

Where is the room 808?
Où est la chambre numéro huit cent huit?
o͞o ē la chombre numēro huit sen̄ huit

The keys, please?
La clé, s'il vous plaît?
lä klē silvo͞o plē

Has anyone asked for me?
Quelqu'un m'a-t-il demandé?
kēlkan mä til demandē

Is there any mail for me?
Y a-t-il du courrier pour moi?
yatil du kuriyer po͞or muwä

Do you have any stamps?
Avez-vous des timbres?
avē vo͞o dē timbr

Where can I get (rent)...............?
Je peux avoir (louer).............où?
s̄e pe avwär (luē)...............o͞o

Could you get me.................?
Pouvez-vous me procurer.................?
p͞oov͞e v͞oo me proqur͞e................

I will be back in ten minutes (a couple of hours)
Je viendrai dans dix minuites (deux heures)
s͞e viyandr͞e dan̄ di min͞et (dezer)

I lost my key.
J'ai perdu la clé.
s͞e p͞erdu lä kl͞e.

What time are the meals served?
Quelles sont les heures de repas?
k͞elson̄ l͞ezer de repä

Can we have breakfast in the room?
Puvons-nous prendre le petit dejeuner dans la chambre?
p͞oovon n͞oo pr͞endr lepet d͞ezhon͞e dan la shambr?

Could I have breakfast at seven tomorrow morning please?
Pouvons nous prendre le petit dejeuner demain à sept heures?
p͞oovon n͞oo prendr le peti d͞ezhon͞e demenä seter?

Please wake me up at 7:30 tomorrow.
Réveillez-moi demain à sept heures.
reveiy͞e-muwä dem͞e ä s͞eter.

Chapter 3

AT THE HOTEL

À l'hôtel:-
Ä Lotēl:-

Customer: Good morning sir, do you have a room please?
Bonjour monsieur, avez-vous une chambre s'il vous plaît?
bonzhur misyu, avē vu yun shombr silvoo plē?

Manager: Yes Madam. We have one beautiful room at the fifth floor and another, small at the second floor.
Oui, madame nous en avons une très jolie au cinquième ètage et une autre petite au deuxième étage.
mēn wi, madäm nu zēn avōn yun tre s̄oli o sēnkiyēm ētazh ē yun otr petit o dozhiyem ētazh.

Customer: I will take that at fifth floor.
Je prendrai celle du cinquième.
zhe prendrai sel du sēnkiyēm.

Manager: How many days would you stay Madam?
Combien de jours pensez-vous rester, madame?
kombiyañ de s̄ur pensē vu rēstē mädäm?

Customer: I don't know yet: two days, one week or a month.
Je ne sais pas encore, deux jours ou une semaine ou un mois.
zhe ne sē pa enkor, de s̄ur yun semen oo uñ mwä.

Manager:	Would you fill up this form? Voulez-vous remplir cette fiche? vulē voo remplir set fiz
Customer:	Yes, why not. Oui, volontiers wi, volontiye.
Manager:	Profession.............teacher. Profession.............institutrice. Profesiyoṉ.............enstitutrise. Name, Sir Name. Nom et prénom: Eh bien, mettons: Michéle Lucienne. noṉ e prēnon: ē byan metoṉ: mishēl Lusiyēn.
Customer:	Nationality...................French. Nationalité...................Française näsyonälitē...................Fransēz. That's all? C'est tout? sē tu?
Manager:	No, madam, you have forgotten to write your address. Non, madame, vous avez oublié d'écrire votre adresse? nō madäm, vuzävē oobliyē dēkrir votr adrēs.
Customer:	Ah! that's right, Its Louis street Los Angeles, that's all. Ah! c'est vrai, la rue St. Louis Los Angeles, voilà. Ah! sē vrē, lā ruy St. Louis Los Angeles vwälä.
Manager:	Thank you, madam. Merci, madame. mērsi, madäm.

Chapter 4

AT THE RESTAURANT

Au restaurant:-
O Rēstoroñ

Is there a good (chinese) restaurant here?
Y a-t-il ici un bon restaurant (restaurant chinois)?
yätil isi ēn boñ restoroñ (restoroñ shinwä)

Would you please reserve a table for four at eight p.m.?
Réservez une table de quatre personnes à 4 heures, sil vous plaît?
rēzervē yun tabl de katr pērson ä 4 her, silvōō plē

Is this table taken?
Cette table est-elle réservée?
sēt tabl ētēl rēzervē

Waiter! / Waitress!
Garçon! / Madame!
gärsoñ! / madäme!

I would like a meal.
Je voudrais commander un plat.
ȝe vudrē komandē en plä.

What can we have right away?
Que pouvez-vous nous servir tout de suite?
ke puvēz vōō nu sērvi tut de swit

Do you have a vegetarian (diet) food too?
Avez-vous aussi des menus végétariens?
ävē voo osi dē mēnu vēzhēteriyeñ

Please bring us one portion of...............
Apportez-nous une...............s'il vous plaît.
aportē-nu yun.............sil voo plē.

A cup (glass, bottle) of...............please.
Une tasse (un verre, une bouteille) de................s'il vous plaît.
yun tās (en vēr, yn botei) de...............sil voo plē.

Chapter 5

LUNCH / DINNER

Dejeuner / Diner
Dēzhonē / Dinē

I would like to have...............
Je voudrais.............
s̄e vōōdrē............

What is the name of this dish?
Comment s'appelle ce plat?
komo sapēl se plä?

Yes, please.
Oui, s'il vous plaît.
wi, sil vōō plē.

Just a little.
Un tout petit peu.
en tut petit pe.

No, thanks.
Non, merci.
nō, mērsi.

Delicious!
Délicieux!
Dēlisiye!

Chapter 6

BANK, CURRENCY EXCHANGE

Where can I change some money?
Où est-ce-que je peux changer de l'argent?
o͞o esk s̄e pe z̄ans̄e de lärseñ

Where is the bank?
Où est la banque?
o͞o ē lä bank

I need a hundred dollars in...............
Je voudrais changer cents dollars en...............
zhe vo͞odrē shans̄e sen dolär eñ...............

How much will I get for...............?
Je touche combien pour...............?
s̄e toosh kombiyan po͞or...............?

Could I have some change please?
Donnez-moi aussi de la monnaie, s'il vous plaît?
Donē-muwa osi dela monē silvo͞o plē?

I would like to cash this cheque.
Je voudrais encaisser ce chèque.
s̄e vo͞odrē enkas̄e se shēk.

Chapter 7

AT THE POST OFFICE

Where is the post office?
Où est le bureau de poste?
o͞o ē le buro de post?

Where is the mail box?
Où est la boîte aux lettres?
o͞o ē la bwät au letre?

How much does this letter cost?
C'est combien pour cette letter?
sē kombiyän po͞or sēt letr?

To the United States. To Canada.
Pour l̄es Etats-Unis. Pour le Canada.
po͞or l̄ezētäz uni. po͞or le canada.

What's the postage on...............
Le tarif postal c'est combien pour...............
le post, sē kombiyan͞ po͞or...............

Five stamps to..........please.
Cinq timbres à...............s'il vous plaît.
sēnk tembr ā..............silvo͞o plē.

Chapter 8

TELEGRAMS, TELEPHONE

A telegram form, please.
Une formule de télégramme, s'il vous plaît.
yun formul de tēlēgram, sil voo plē.

I would like to send...............a telegram.
Je voudrais envoyer...............un télégramme.
zhe voodrē envoyē...............en tēlēgram.

How much do ten words to...............cost?
Combien coûtent dix-mots pour...............?
kombiyañ kut di-mo poor...............?

Will the wire get to...............today?
Le télégramme arrivera encore aujourd hui à...............?
le tēlēgram arivera enkor oōordwi?

Where is the phone booth, please?
Où est la cabine téléphonique?
oō e lä käbin tēlēfonik

The phone-book, please.
L'annuaire (du téléphone) s'il vous plaît.
lanuyer (du tēlēfon) sil voō plē.

Can I direct dial to...............?
Je peu faire un numéro interurbain automatique?
še pe fēr en numēro enterurbēn otomatik?

What is the area code for...............?
Quel est l'indicatif pour...............?
kēlē lēndikatif poor...............?

Can I have some coins for the pay phone?
Avez-vous des jetons pour le taxiphone?
avē-voo dē zheton poor le taksifon?

How much does a local call cost?
Combien coûte une communication urbaine?
kombiyan kut yun komunikasiyon erbēn?

What time does the night rate begin?
Le tarif de nuit, c'est à partir de quelle heure?
le tarif de nui sēta parti de keler?

What is your number?
Quel est votre numéro?
kēlē votr numēro?

Wrong number!
C'est un faux numéro.
sētan fo numēro.

Chapter 9

GOING SHOPPING

Where can I get (buy)...............?
Où est-ce que je peux trouver (acheter)...............?
o͞o e̅sk ʒe pe truve̅ (ashete)...............?

I need...............
J'ai besion de...............
zhe̅ be̅swañ de...............

Is there a leather shop here?
Y a-t-il un magasin de cuir?
ya til en megaze̅n de kwir?

Have you got...............?
Avez-vous...............?
ave̅-voo...............?

I want...............
Je voudrais...............
ʒe vo͞odre̅...............

Please show me...............
Montrez-moi...............s'il vous plaît.
montre̅ mwä sil vo͞o ple̅.

Please give me...............
Donnez-moi...............s'il vous plaît.
done̅-mwä...............sil vo͞o ple̅.

That's plenty.
C'est assez.
sē asē.

Can I exchange it?
Je peux l'échanger?
zhe pe lēzänsē?

I don't like the shape.
Je n'aime pas la forme.
 ̄se nēmpa lā form.

I like that.
Cela me plaît.
sēla me plē.

I will take it.
Je le (la, les) prends.
 ̄se le (lā, lē) prēn.

How much is that?
Ça coûte combien?
sä kōōt kombiyän?

Do you take credit cards (traveller's cheques)?
Vous acceptez des cartes de credit (des chêques de voyage)?
vōōzavē äksēptē dē kärt krēdi (dē shēk de voyazhe)

Part-IX
Chapter 1

BASIC FRENCH GRAMMAR RULES

I. The Articles

1. There are two genders in French, masculine and feminine.
2. The definite article in the masculine singular is le (le) eg. le livre [le livr] the book.
3. The definite article in the feminine singular is la (lä) eg. lā maison [lä mēzon] the house.
4. The masculine and feminine plural is always les (lē). eg. les livres [lē livr] the books. Les maisons [lē mezoṉ] the houses.
5. The indifinite article in the feminine singular is un [en] eg. un cheval [en shēval] a horse.
6. The indifinite article in the feminine singular is une (yun) eg. une lettre [yun lētr] a letter.
7. Nouns expressing an indefinite amount or indifinite number of items take the partitive which is formed by the preposition de and the definite article. eg. du pain. [du pēn] bread, de la viande [de lä viyand] meat, des amis [dē zami] friends. There is no English equivalent for the partitive.

II. The Noun

1. As in English, the subject and object function of the noun is indicated by its place in the sentence.
2. The possessive case can be indicated by <u>de</u> [de] or <u>à</u> [ä].

3. <u>de</u> and à are combined with le and les in the following ways:
   de le becomes du [du] meaning of the/from the
   de les becomes des [dē] meaning of the/from the
   à le becomes au [o] meaning to the/at the
   à les becomes aux [ō] meaning to the/at the

III. The Adjectives and the adverb

1. The adjectives agree in number and gender with the nouns they modify.
2. Adverbs are formed by adding — ment to the feminine form of the adjective.
3. The feminine form of the adjective is formed by adding <u>e</u> to the maculine (m) form (if this does not already end in <u>e</u>).

   eg. m grand (grän)
       f grande (gränd).

IV. Comparison

1. The comparative is formed by placing plus [plu] more, before the adjective or adverb e.g. beau [bo] beautiful.

   plus beau [plu bo] more beautiful.
   rapidement [räpidmeñ] fast.
   plus rapidement [plu räpidmeñ] faster.

2. The superlative adjectives and adverbs is formed by placing the definite article before the comparative. e.g. le plus beau voyage. [le plu bo voyäzh] the most beautiful trip.

V. Formation of Plurals

1. As in English, the plural is generally formed by adding <u>s</u> to the singular noun.

   e.g. le livre [le livr] the book.
        les livers [lē livr] the books.

2. Nouns ending in s, x and z do not change in plural.

   e.g. la souris [lä sōōris] the mouse.
   les souris [lē sōōris] the mice.

3. Most nouns ending in à and some nouns ending <u>ail</u> form the plural by <u>aux</u>.

   e.g. le cheval [le shēval] the horse.
   les chevaux [lē shevo] the horses.

VI. Pronouns
Personal Pronouns:

(a) <u>Subject Pronouns</u>

je	[zhe]	I	nous	[nōō]	we
tu	[tu]	you	vous	[vōō]	you
il	[il]	he	ils	[il]	they (m)
elle	[el]	she	elles	[el]	they (f)

(b) <u>Direct and Indirect object Pronouns. The conjunctive personal Pronouns are</u>

Indirect Object

me	[me]	me
te	[te]	you
lui	[luwi]	him, it
lui	[luwi]	her, it
se	[se]	youself, himself hereself, itself
nous	[nōō]	us
vous	[vōō]	you (pl)
leur	[ler]	them

Direct Object

me	[me]	me
te	[te]	you
le	[le]	him, it
la	[lä]	her, it
se	[se]	himself, yourself herself, itself
nous	[nōō]	us
vous	[vōō]	you (pl)
les	[lē]	them (m)
les	[lē]	them (f)

In general, these personal pronouns precede the verb. e.g. il me donne [il me done] He gives me.

(c) <u>Possessive Pronouns</u>
Adjective function (preceding a noun) Masculine.

Mon [moñ] my
Ton [toñ] your
Son [soñ] his/her

Feminine.
Ma [mä] my
Ta [tä] your
Sa [sä] his/her
Notre [notr] our
Votre [votr] your
Leur [ler] their

Plural (masculine and feminine)
Mes [mē] my
Tes [tē] your
Ses [sē] his/her
Nos [no] ours
Vos [vo] yours
Leurs [lerz] theirs

(d) <u>Demonstrative Pronouns</u>
Ce [se] this
Cet [sēt] this
Cette [sētt] this
Ces [sē] these

(e) <u>Relative Pronouns</u>
   Qui   [ki]   who (persons), which that (things)
   dont   [doñ]   of whom, about whom, of which
   à qui [ā ki]   to whom
   qui   [ki]   whom (person) which, that.

(f) Interrogative Pronouns
   Quel   [kēl]   what? / which? (m / sing)
   Quels   [kēl]   what? / which? (m / plural)
   quelle [kēl]   what? / which? (f / plural)
   quelles [kēl]   what? / which? (f / plural)

Verbs

The most important tenses are

(a) The Present Tense

It expresses actions and situations taking place in the present:
Nicolas regarde son père.
Nicolas is looking at his father.

(b) The Future Tense

It expresses actions and situations taking place in the future:
Demain nous partirons en vacances.
Tomorrow we are going on vacation.

(c) The Past Tense

It expresses actions and situations which have already occured in the past:
Je suis allé au cinéma.
I went to the cinema.

Quick & Easy Way to Learn French / 121

<u>In French the verbs are of 2 types</u>
(a) Irregular verbs as they do not follow the set pattern of conjugation.
(b) Regular verbs as they follow the set pattern of conjugation.

Conjugation of Irregular Verbs Avoir and être:-

	Present	**Past**	**Future**
Avoir = to have			
j	ai	eu	aurai
tu	as	eu	auras
Il	a	eu	aura
Elle	a	eu	aura
Nous	avons	eu	aurons
Vous	avez	eu	aurez
Ils	ont	eu	auront
Elles	ont	eu	auront
Être = to be			
je	suis	allé	serai
tu	es	allé	seras
Il	est	allé	sera
Elle	est	allée	sera
Nous	sommes	allés	serons
Vous	êtes	allés	serez
Ils	sont	allés	seront
Elles	sont	allées	seront

Regular Verbs

In French verbs are classified by their infinitive endings:-
1. Verbs ending in — er
2. Verbs ending in — ir
3. Verbs ending in — re

Most verbs belong to the first group

	ER	**IR**	**RE**
Infinitive	Donner (give)	Finir (finish)	Mettre (put)
Present Tense	je donne	je finis	je mets
	tu donnes	tu finis	tu mets
	il donne	il finit	il met
	elle donne	elle finit	elle met
	nous donnons	nous finissons	nous mettons
	vous donnez	vous finissez	vous mettez
	ils donnent	ils finissent	ils mettent
	elles donnent	elles finissent	elles mettent

Negative Sentences

The negative is expressed by using the word **ne** together with another word **pas**, **plus** etc.

1. not: ne..........pas.
   Ce n'est pas mon manteau. This is not my coat.
2. Nothing / not anything: ne.........rien.
   Il n'a rien à manger. He has nothing to eat.
3. Nobody / not anything: ne.........personne.
   Je n'y ai vu personne. I saw nobody there.
4. Never: ne........jamais.
   Il ne fait jamais la tasse. He never washes cup.

Interrogative Sentences

How to ask questions

There are generally three ways to form interrogative sentences.

1. <u>Using the word Est-ce-que.</u>
   Est-ce-que tu es contente?
   Are you happy?
2. <u>Transposing the subject and Verb.</u>
   Es-tu contente?
   Are you Happy?
3. <u>Using rising inflection at the end of the sentence.</u>
   Tu es contente?
   Are you happy?

Interrogative Pronouns:-

The most important interrogative pronouns are.

When	quand	koñ?
Why	pourquoi	pōōrkwa?
What	qu'est-ce-que	kēske?
Which	quel / quelle (f)	kēl
Who	à qui	ä ki
Who	qui	ki
How	comment	komoñ
How long	combien de temps	kombiyañ de temp
How much	combien	kombiyañ
Where	où	ōō
What...of	à quoi	ä kwa
What...about	de quoi	de kwa
Whom...about	de qui	de ki

TOOLS

outil:-
ooti:-

English	French	Pronunciation
Air pump	pompe à air	pomp ä ēr
Bolt	vis	vis
Boltnut	écrou	ēkroo
Cable	câble	käbl
Chisel	ciseau	sizo
Cloth	chiffon	shifoñ
Drill	foret	forē
Funnel	etonnoir	ētonwar
Hammer	marteau	marto
Jack	cric	krik
Pliers	tenailles	tenaiyē
Sand paper	papier verré	papiyē verē
Screw	vis	vis
Screw driver	tournveuis	toornvis
Tool	outil	ōoti
Tool box	coffre à outil	kofr ä ōoti
Wire	fil métallique	fil mētalik
Wrench	clé anglaise	klē anglēz

AT THE BUS STOP

ā l'autobus:-
ā lotobus:-

Where is the bus stop?
Où est l'arrèt l'antobus?
o͞o ē lārē dotobyus?

Where do the buses to..........stop?
Où s'arrêtent les autobus pour..........?
o͞o sarēte lē zotobus?

Is that far?
Est-ce loin?
ē se luwañ?

When does a (first/last) bus leave for?
Quand part un (le première/dernier) autobus pour..........?
kon pär en le (premiyēr/derniyer) otobus po͞or..........?

Which bus goes to..........?
Quel autobus va à..........?
kēl otobus vä ä..........?

Is there a bus to..........?
Y a-t-il un autobus pour..........?
yatil en otobus po͞or..........?

When do we get to..........?
Quand arrivons-nous à..........?
kon arivoñ no͞o ä..........?

Do I have to change buses for..........?
Faut-il changer d'autobus pour..........?
fotil z̄anz̄e dotobus po͞or..........?

Where do I have to change?
Où faut-il changer?
o͞o fotil shanze?

One (two) round-trip ticket(s) please.
Un ticket (deux ticket) aller et retour pour.
en tike̅ (de tike̅) ale̅ e̅ reto͞or po͞or.

One full-fare and one half-fare to..........please.
Un ticket et une demi-place pour..........s'il vous plaît.
en tike̅ fer e̅ yun demi-place po͞or..........silvo͞ople̅.

ON BUS

En autobus:-
en otobus:-

Bus	autobus	otobus
Bus terminal	terminus	terminus
Direction	direction	dire̅ksiyon̄
Driver	conducteur	konducter
Luggage	bagages	baga̅s̄
Route	ligne	linye
Stop	arrêt	är̄e
Ticket	ticket/billet	tike̅/biye̅
Transfer	ticket de-correspondance	tike̅ de-korespondonse

AT THE STATION

à la gare:-
ä lä gär:-

English	French	Pronunciation
Arrival/departure	arrivée/départ	ärivē/dēpar
Connection	correspondance	korespondons
Sleeper	couchettes	kōōshēt
Dining car	wagon restaurant	wägon restoroṉ
Express train	train direct	trēn dirēkt
Fast train	rapide	räpid
Motorail service	train	trēn
Platform	quai	vo kai
Rail car	automotrice	otomotris
Sleeper/sleeping car	wagon-lit	wägon-li
Time-table	indicateur chaix	endikater shē
Track	voie	vwä
Round trip	aller retour	aēe retōōr
One way	aller simple	alē simple
First class	première	premiyēr
Second class	de seconde	de segōnd
Fare	prix de billet	pri de biyē
Half fare	demi-place	demi-pläs

AT THE STATION INFORMATION

à la gare:-
ä lä gār:-

When is there a local (express) train to..........?
Quand part un train omnibus (express) pour..........?
koñ pār en trēn omnibus (exprē) poor..........?

Is this the train to..........?
Est-ce le train pour..........?
ēs le trēn poor..........?

Does this train go by the way of..........?
Ce train passe par..........?
se trēn pas pär..........?

How much late?
Combien?
kombiyañ?

When does it get to..........?
Quand arrive-t-il à..........?
koñ arrive til ä..........?

Do we have to change trains?
Faut-il changer de train?
fotil shanzhē de trēn?

What platform does the train from..........come in on?
Sur quel quai arrive le train de..........?
sur kēl kai arive le trēn de..........?

What platform does the train for..........leave from?
De quel quai part le train pour..........?
de kēl kai pär le trēn pōor..........?

PORTER

Porteur:-
porter:-

Please bring this luggage to the train.
Apporte ces bagages s'il vous plaît au train pour..........
äporte sē bagās silvōoplē au trēn pōor..........

To the baggage check area.
à la consigne.
ä lä koñsen.

To the exit.
à la sortie.
ä lä sorti.

To the taxi.
Au taxi.
o taxi

To the..........bus.
à l'autobus..........pour.
ā lotobus..........pōor.

How much does that cost?
Ça coûte combien?
sa kōot kombiyañ?

ON THE PLATFORM

à la gare:-
ä lä gäre:-

Is this the train to..........?
Est-ce le train pour..........?
ēs le trēn pōor..........?

Where is..........?
Où est..........?
ōō ē..........?

First class?
La première classe?
lä promiyēr klas?

The luggage car?
Le fourgon?
le fōorzhon?

Car number..........?
La voiture numéro..........?
lä vwatur numēro..........?

The sleeping car?
Le wagon lit?
le vagoṅ li?

What time does the train arrive?
À quelle heure arrive le train?
ä kēler ärive le trēn?

AT THE BORDER

Au board:-
ō bord:-

When do we get to the border?
Quand arriverons-nous à la frontière?
koṅ arriveroṅ-noo ä la frontiyer?

Your passport, please.
Votre passeport, s'il vous plaît.
votr pasport sil vo͞o plē.

Your papers please.
Vos papiers s'il vous plaît.
vō päpiyē sil vo͞o plē.

Here they are.
Tenez s'il vous plaît.
tenē sil vo͞o plē.

I will be staying a week.
Je resterai une semaine.
z̄e resterē yun semēn.

I am here on business.
C'est un voyage d'affaires.
sēten voyäs̄ däfēr.

CUSTOMS CONTROL

Do you have anything to declare?
Avez-vous quelquechose à déclarer?
ävē voo kelke shoz ä dēklarē?

I only have articles for my personal use.
Je n'ai que des objets personnels.
s̄e nē ke dēzobzhē pērsonēl.

That isn't mine.
Ce n'est pas à moi.
se nēpaza muwa.

Please open.
Ouvrez..........s'il vous plaît.
oovrē sil voo plē.

This is a present (souvenir).
C'est un cadeaux (souvenir de voyage).
sēten kädo (soovenir de voyas̄)

I have cigarettes (a bottle of perfume).
J'ai des cigarettes (du perfum).
s̄edē sigärēt (du perfum).

That's my suitcase.
C'est ma valise.
sē mä valise.

What is in here?
Qu'est ce-qu'il y a là dedans?
kēskilya lä dedan̄?

I would like to declare this.
Je voudrais déclarer ça.
zhe voodrē dēklarē sa.

That's all.
C'est tout.
sē too.

Alright!
D'accord.
däkor.

Do I have to pay duty on this?
Dois-je déclarer ça?
dwa-s̄e dēklarē sa?

IN THE STREET

Dans la rue:-
don lā riyu:-

Where is........?
Où est..........?
oo ē..........?

English	French	Pronunciation
The bus stop	l'arrêt d'autobus	larēt dotobus
Catholic Church	l'eglise catholique	lēgliz catholik
City Hall	l'hotel de ville	lotēl de vil
Harbour	port	por
The ......Hotel	l' hôtel	lotēl

Museum	musée	muzē
Police Station	commissariat de police	komisariyä de polis
Post office	bureau de poste	byuro de post
Street	rue	ryu
Station	gare	gär
Taxi stand	station de taxi	stäsiyoñ de taxi

Is it far from here?
Est-ce loin d'ici?
ēs luwañ disi

How far is it to the..........?
Quelle est la distance d'ici au..........?
kēlē la distans disi o..........

How many minutes by foot?
Combien de minuites à pied?
kombiyañ de minuit ā piyē

A good distance. (Not far).
Assez (Pas) loin.
asē (pa) luwañ.

Which direction is..........?
Dans quelle direction se trouve..........?
doñ kēl dirēksiyoñ se trōōve..........?

What street is..........on?
Dans quelle rue se trouve..........?
doñ kēl ryu se trōōve..........?

There.
Là.
lä.

Straight ahead.
Tout droit.
tōō drwä.

To the right.
À droite.
ä drwät

To the left.
À gauche.
ä goz̄.

AEROPLANE

L'avion:-
läviyōn̄:-

English	French	Pronunciation
Aircraft	avion	aviyōn̄
Air passenger	voyageur	voyās̄er
Airport	aéroport	ēropor
Airport- service charge	taxe d'aéroport	tax dēropor
Air sickness	mal de l'air	mäl de l̄er
Arrival	arrivée	ärivē
Charter plane	charter	sharter
Crew	équipage	ēquipäs̄
Destination	destination	dēstinasiyōn̄
Duty free	marchandises	märz̄andiz
Goods	hors-taxe	hor-täx

English	French	Pronunciation
Emergency exit	sortie de secours	sorti de sekōor
Emergency landing	atterisage forcé	aterisaś forsē
Engine	réacteur	reyakter
Excess baggage	exédent de bagages	ēxēden de bagäś
Flight	vol	vol
Flight attendant	hôtesse de l'air	hotēs de lēr
Flying time	durée de vol	durē de vol
Fog	brouillard	bruiyär
Gate	pont-d'embarquement	pon-dembarkmeñ
Hand luggage	bagage à main	bagäś ä meñ
Helicopter	hélicoptère	hēlikopter
Information	information	enformēsiyoñ
Information-counter	guichet-d'information	guishē-denformēsiyoñ
Immediate landing	escale	ēskäl
Land	atterir	äterir
Landing	atterrıssage	äterisaś
Life jacket	gilet de sauvetage	gilē de sovetäzh
Pilot	commandent de bord	komondoñ de bord
Plain	avion	äviyoñ
Return flight	vol de retour	vol de retōor
Route	ligne arienne	lin aēriyen
Scheduled flight	vol régulier	vol rēguliyē
Seat belt	ceinture	sēntyur
Take off	départ	dēpar
Thunderstorm	orage	oräś
Ticket	billet d'avion	biyē d'aviyoñ
Waiting room	salle d'attente	säl dätente
Wing	aile	aiy

AT THE AIRPORT

A l'aeroport:-
ä leroport:-

Can I take this along as hand luggage?
Puis-je prendre cela comme bagage à main?
puyi zhe prend sēla kom bägäzh ä main?

Where is the visiting room (Exit B, Gate B)?
Où est la salle d'attente (la sortie B)?
oo ē lä säl dätont (la sorti B)A

Where is the information counter?
Où sont les renseignements?
oo son lē ronsenmon?

Where is the duty-free shop?
Où peut-on acheter des marchandises hors-taxe?
oo peton äshetē dē märshondiz hor tax?

Is the plane to..........late?
L'appareil pour..........a du retard?
läperai poor............a du retard?

Is the plane to..........late?
L'appareil pour..........du retard.
läpereyi poor..........du rētard?

Has the plane from..........already landed?
L'avion venant de..........a-t-il déja atterri?
läviyon venonde..........ätil dēzha āteri?

How high are we flying?
À quelle altitude sommes-nous?
ä kel altitude som n̄o͞o

Where are we now?
Où sommes-nous maintenant?
o͞o som-n̄o͞o mētno

Please fasten your seat belts!
Attachez vos ceintures!
ätäshē vo ciyantur

Can I have..........?
Je peux avoir..........?
že pe awar..........

I feel sick.
J'ai mal au coeur.
že mäl o ker.

When do we land?
Quand atterrissons-nous?
kon äterisoñ-n̄o͞o

How is the weather in..........?
Quel temps fait-il à..........?
kēl tomp fetil ä..........

BY AIR
(INFORMATION & RESERVATIONS)

En avion:-
en äviyon:-

Is there a (direct) flight to..........?
Y a-t-il un vol (direct) pour..........?
yatil en vol (dirēkt) poor..........

Is there a connection to..........?
J' y a une correspondance pour..........?
sē yun korrespondoñs poor..........

When is there a plane today (tomorrow) to..........?
Quand part le prochain appareil pour..........?
kon par le proshēn äperei poor..........

Does the plane take a stopover in..........?
L'appareil fait escale à..........?
läperai fē eskäl ä..........

When do we get to..........?
À quelle heure sevons-nous à..........?
ä kēler seroñ noo ä..........

How much is a (round-trip) flight to..........?
Combien coûte un vol (aller et retour) à..........?
kombiyan koot en vol (ălē ē retoor) ā..........

What are the luggage charges?
À combien de bagages a-t-on droit?
ä kombiyañ de bagäzh äton drwä

How much does excess baggage cost?
Les bagages en exédent, c'est combien?
lē bägäs en exēden sē kombiyan?

How much is the airport service charge?
La taxe d'aéroport, c'est combien?
lā tax dēroport sē kombiyan?

How do I get to the airport?
Pour aller à l'aeroport?
pōōr älē ā leroport?

I would like to reserve a seat on Friday night to..........?
Je voudrais faire une reservation pour un vol pour..........vendredi
S.V.P. (s'il vous plaît)
zhe vōōdrē fēr yun rēzervasiyon pōōr en vol poor..........vendredi
S.V.P. (sil vōō plē)

First class.
Première classe.
premiyēr klas.

Economy class.
Classe économique.
klas ekonomik.

How much does it cost?
Combien dois-je payer?
kombiyan dwä se pēyē?

How long is the ticket valid?
Quelle est la durée de validité du billet d'avion?
kelē la durē de validitē du biyē daviyon?

I have to cancel my reservation?
Il me faut annuler (changer) la réservation?
il me fō anyulē (zansē) la rēzervasiyon?

What is the cancellation fee?
La taxe d'annulation, c'est combien?
la tax danulasiyon sē kombiyan?

BUS, TAXI

L'autobus/taxi:-
lotobus/täxi:-

Can I get there by bus?
Je peux y aller en autobus?
zhe pe i älē en otobus?

Which bus goes to..........?
Combien d'arrêts y a-t-il?
kombiyan darēt yatil?

Where do I have to get out (change)?
Où faut-il descendre (changer d'autobus)?
ōō fotil dēsendr (zansē dotobus)?

Would you please tell me when to get these?
Dites-moi quand nous serons à..........s'il vous plaît?
dit-muwä kon nōō seron ä..........sil vōō plē?

A one-way ticket to..........
Un billet simple pour..........
ēn biyē sēmpl pōōr..........

Where can I get a taxi?
Je peux prendre un taxi où?
s̄e pe prendr en tāxi o͞o?

Take me to..........
Conduisez-moi au..........
konduizē muwa ō..........

To the station, please.
À la gare, s'il vous plaît.
ä lä gär sil vo͞o plē.

How much is the fare to..........?
Ça fait combien..........?
sa fē kombiyan..........?

Could you show us one of the sights?
Pourriez-vous nous montrer quelques attractions touristiques?
puriyē-vo͞o no͞o montrē kelk zaträksyon to͞oristik?

Please wait (stop) here a minute?
Attendez ici un moment, s'il vous plaît?
ätendē isi en momo, sil vo͞o plē?

SIGHTSEEING AND EXCURSIONS

Les dialogues:-
lē diyälog

English	French	Pronunciation
Castle	château	shäto
Cathedral	cathédrale	kathēdral

Church	l'église	lēgliz
Fortress	forteresse	forterēs
Exhibition	exposition	ēxpozisiyon̄
Gallary	galérie	gäleri
Memorial	monument-commémoratif	monumon̄ komēmoratif
Museum	musée	myuzē
Palace	palais	pälē
Zoo	zoo	zoo
Amusement-park	parc-d'attractions	park-datraksiyon̄
Area	région	rēsyon̄
Boat trip	promenade en bateau	promēnade en bäto
Botanical-gardens	jardin-botanique	zharden-botanik
Bridge	pont	pon̄
Capital	capitale	kapitäl
Cave	caverne	kävern
City	ville	vil
Consulate	consulat	konsulät
Cornet	coin	kwan̄
Countryside	paysage	pēyēsazh
Deadend street	voie sans issue	vwa son isyu
District	région	rēsyon̄
Ditch	fosée	fosē
Embassy	ambassade	embäsäd
Excavations	fouilles	foiyē
Excursion	excursion	exkersiyon̄
Factory	usine	uzin
Farm house	ferme	fērm

Fire department	pompiers	pompiyē
Fountain	fontaine	fontēn
Garden	jardin	zhärden
Gate	portail	portäy
Government office	administration	administrasiyoñ
Grave	tombe	tōmb
Harbour	port	por
High-rise building	tour	tōor
Hill	colline	kolin
House	maison	mēzon
House number	numéro de la maison	numēro de lä mēzon
Landscape	paysage	pēyēsäzh
Last stop	terminus	terminus
Library	bibliothèque	bibliyotēk
Lost and found-office	bureau des-objets trouvés	buro dēz-obzhē trōovē
Military base	base militère	base militer
Ministry	ministère	minister
Montain	montagne	montän
Montain range	chaine de montagnes	shēn de montän
National park	parc national	park nasiyonäl
Pavilion	pavillon	paviloñ
Policeman	agent de police	azhent de police
Police station	commissariat de-police	komisariyē-de poliçe
River	fleuve	flev
Road	rue	ryu
School	école	ē kol

Shop	magasin	magazen
Shopping mall	centre commercial	sentr komersial
Swimming area	piscine	pisin
Taxi	taxi	taxi
Taxi stand	station de taxi	stasiyoñ de täxi
Temple	temple	templ
Tomb	tombe	tomb
Tower	tour	tōor
Town	ville	vil
Traffic	circulation	sērkuläsyoñ
Traffic light	feux	fe
Travel agency	agence de voyage	aseñ de voyäs
University	université	univērsitē
Valley	vallée	valē
Village	village	villäs
Wall	mur	myur
Waterfall	cascade	käskäd
Zebra crossing	passage clouté	päsäs klutē
Zoo	zoo	zoo

Two tickets for the..........tomorow, please.
Pour demain deux places pour..........s'il vous plaît.
pōor demēn de plas pōor..........sil vōo plē.

Is lunch included?
Est-ce que le déjeuner est compris?
esk le dēzhonē ē kompri?

Where (when) do we meet?
Où (quand) nous retrouvons-nous?
ōo (kon) nōo retrōovon-nōo?

When do we get going?
Quelle est l'heure du départ?
kēlēr du dēpar?

Will we be seeing the..........too?
Visitons-nous aussi..........?
vizition-noo ossi..........?

How much?
Combien?
kombiyan̄?

When do we get back?
Quand rentrons..........nous?
kon retreron̄..........noo?

When does..........open (close)?
ä quelle heure ouvre (ferme)..........?
ä kēler oovr (ferm)..........?

Will we have some free time.
Avons-nous du temps à notre disposition?
Avon-noo du tomp ā notr disposition?

Will we be able to do some shopping?
On peut faire du shopping?
on-pe fēr du shopping?

How long will we stay in............?
Combien de temps resterons-nous à..........?
kombiyan de tomp resteron-noo ä ....?

What's worth seeing in..........?
Quelles curiosités y-a-t- il à..........?
kēl qurisositē yatil ā..........?

How much does the admission cost?
Combien coûte l'entrée?
kombiyan cōōt lentrē?

Is there an English-speaking guide?
Y-at-il un guide qui parle anglais?
yatil en gid ki parle englē?

I would like to see the..........
J' aimerais voir..........
sēmerē vwar..........

Can we take a look at..........today?
Peut-on visiter aujourd' hui?
petoñ visitē ozhordwi?

When does the tour start?
A quelle heure commence la visite guidée?
ä kēler komonse lä vizite guidē?

Can we take pictures?
On peut faire des photos?
onpe fēr dē foto?

What is that building (monument)?
Quel édifice (monument) est- ce?
kēl ēdifis (monumon) ēs?

Who painted this picture?
De qui est ce tableau?
de ki ē se tablo?

What period does this..............date from?
De quel siècle est..........?
de kēl siekl ē..........?

When was..........built?
Quand a été bâti?
kon ä ētē bati?

Where can I find..........?
Où se trouve..........?
ōō se trōōv..........?

Who built..........?
Qui a bâti..........?
ki ä bäti..........?

Is this..........?
Est-ce-que c'est..........?
esk sē..........?

GOING SHOPPING

Faire des affaires:-
fer dezafer:-

Where can I get..........?
Où est-ce-que je peux trouver..........?
o͞o e͞sk zhe pe tro͞ove͞..........?

I need..........
J'ai besoin de..........
zhe͞ be͞swan de..........

Is there a leather shop here?
Y a-t-il un magasin de cuir?
yatil e͞n megazen de quir?

Have you got..........?
Avez-vous..........?
ave͞ vo͞o..........?

I would (we'd) like..........
Je voudrais (nous voudrions)..........
s͞e vo͞odre͞ (no͞o vo͞odriyon)..........

Please show me..........
Montrez-moi s'il vous plaît..........
montre͞-muwa sil vo͞o ple͞..........

Please give me..........
Donnez-moi s'il vous plaît.
done͞-muwa sil vo͞o ple͞.

That's plenty.
C'est assez.
sētasē.

A little more.
Encore un peu.
Enkor eñpe.

Can you order it for me?
Pouvez-vous le commander?
poōvē-voo le komondē?

When will you get it in?
Quand est-ce que vous l'aurez?
kon esk voo lōrē?

Can I exchange it?
je peux l'échanger?
ѯe pe lēshanzhē?

I don't like the shape (colour).
La forme (couleur) ne me plaît pas.
la form (coōler) ne me plē pa.

This is not enough.
Ce n'est pas assez.
Se nēpa zasē.

Have you got something little nicer (less expensive)?
Vous avez quelque chose de mieux (de moins cher)?
voōzavē kēlkeshoz de miye (de muwa shēr)?

I like that.
Ça me plaît.
sa me plē.

I will take it.
Je le (la, les) prends.
 ͞se le (lā, lē) pron̄.

How much is that?
Ça coûte combien?
sa co͞ot kombiyan̄?

Thanks, that'll be all.
Merci, c'est tout.
mēhsi, sētu.

Can you send my stuff to the..........hotel please?
Pouvez-vous m'envoyer la merchandise à l'hôtel..........s'il vous plaît?
po͞ovē-vo͞o menvoyē la mershandiz ä lotēl sil vo͞o plē?

Do you take credit cards (traveller's cheques)?
Vous acceptez des cartes de credit (des chèques de voyage)?
vo͞oz akseptē dē kart de credit. (dē shak dē voyazh)?

Vocabulaire:-
vokabulēr:-

English	French	Pronunciation
Bag	sac	säk
Bottle	bouteille	boteiy
Box	boîte	bwät

Few	quelques	kēlk
Jar	verre	vēr
Pound	livre	livr
Pack (packet)	paquet	pakē
Pair	paire	pēr
Piece	morceau	morso
Roll	rouleau	rulo
Tube	tube	tub
Two pounds	kilo	kilo
Yard	mètre	mētr
Antique shop	magasin d'antiquités	magazēn dentikitē
Bakery	boulangerie	bulonzheri
Barber shop	coiffeur	kwäfer
Beauty parlour	institut de beauté	enstitut de butē
Book shop	librairie	librēri
Butcher shop	boucherie	bōōsheri
Candy store	confiserie	konfiseri
China shop	magasin de-porcelaine	magāzēn-de porselēn
Cigar store	bureau de tabac	buro de täbä
Cobbler shop	cordonnerie	kordoneri
Cosmetic salon	institut de beauté	enstitut de butē
Department store	grand magasin	gron magazēn
Dressmaker's shop	tailleur pour dames	taiyer pōōr däm
Drug store	droguerie	drogeri
Chemist	pharmacie	farmäsi
Dry cleaner's	nettoyage	netoyäs̄
Electrical shop	magasin-d'électroménager	magazēn-dēlēktromē nazhēr

Fish market	poissonnerie	pwasoneri
Flower shop	magasin de fleurs	magazēn de flur
Fruit market	epicerie marché	ēpiseri marshē
Furniture store	magasin de meubles	mogäzēn de mubl
Grocery store	épicerie	ēpiseri
Hardware store	quincaillerie	kinkaleri
Hat shop	chapellerie	shapeleri
Jewellery shop	bijouterie	bizhōōteri
Laundry	blanchisserie	blanz̄isri
Leather goods store	maroquinerie	marokineri
Lingerie shop	magasin de l'ingerie	magazēn de lenzheri
Liquor store	vins et spiriteux	vēn ē spirito
Music store	magasin de musique	magazēn de muzik
News dealer	merchand de journaux	marshand- de zhōōrno
Optician	opticien	optisiyeñ
Perfume shop	parfumerie	parfumeri
Pet shop	magasin d'animaux	magazen d'animo
Photo shop	photographe	fotogräf
Poultry shop	commerce de volailles	komerse de voläyel
Real estate agency	agence immobilière	asens imobiliēr
Second hand book- shop	librairie d'occasion	librēri dokäzyon
Shoe store	magasin- de chaussure	magazēn- de z̄osyur
Souvenir shop	magasin de souvenir	magäzeñ de sōōvenir
Sports goods store	magasin de sport	magäzeñ de sport
Stationery store	papeterie	papēteri
Tailor shop	tailleur	taiyē

Toy store	magasin de jouets	magaz̄en de zhuiyēt
Vegetable market	marchand de légumes	märz̄añ de lēgume
Watch maker's shop	horlogerie	horlozheri
Wine shop	marchand de vin	märz̄añ de vēn

FLOWERS

Fleur:-
flur:-

English	French	Pronunciation
Bouquet	bouquet	bōōkē
Chrysanthemums	chrysanthèmes	krisēnthēm
Flower pot	pot de fleurs	pōt de flur
Flowers	fleurs	flur
Lilacs	lilas	lilä
Orchids	orchidées	orshidē
Roses	roses	roze
Tulips	tulipes	tulip
Vase	vase	väs
Violets	violettes	viyolēt

BOOK SHOP

*Librairie:-
libreri:-*

English	French	Pronunciation
Autobiography	autobiographie	otobiyografi
Biography	biographie	biyografi
Book	livre	livr
Catalogue	catalogue	katalog
Children's book	livre pour enfants	livr poor enfañ
City map	plan de la ville	plän de lä vil
Detective novel	roman policier	romēn polisiyē
Dictionary	dictionnaire	diksiyonēr
Guide book	guide touristique	gid tōoristik
Map	carte géographique	kart zhiyografik
Novel	roman	romēn
Paper back	livre de poche	livr de poz̄
Phrase book	guide de-conversation	gid de-konvorsasiyoñ
Poetry book	recueil de poésie	rekei de poēzi
Record	disque	disk
Road map	carte routière	kart rutiyēr
Story book	livre de contes	livr de kont
Text book	manuel	mänuēl
Translation	traduction	träduksiyoñ
Travel reading	lecture de voyage	lēktur de voyās̄
Volume	volume	volyum

PHOTOSHOP

Would you please develop this film?
Développez-moi ce rouleau, s'il vous plaît?
dēvelopē-muwa se rulo sil vōō plē?

One print of each negative, please.
Une épreuve de chaque négatif, s'il vous plaît.
Yun ēprev de zäk nēgatf silvōō plē.

Three by four (inches).
Sept (sur) dix.
sēt sur di.

I would like..........
Je voudrais..........
ʒe vōōdrē..........

A cartridge file.
Un film à châssis.
en film ä châssis.

Would you please put the film in camera please?
Vous pourriez me mettre la pellicule dans l'appareil, s'il vous plaît?
vōō puriyē me mētr la pēliqul don laparayi sil vōō plē?

VOCABULARY

English	French	Pronunciation
Camera	appareil photographique	apērayi photografik
Colour Film	pellicule en couleurs.	péliqule ēn coōler
Develop	développer	devlopē
Development	dévoloppement	dēvolopmen
Diaphragm	diaphragme	daiyafram
Exposure	exposition	Expozisiyoṉ
Film	film / pellicule	film/pēliqul
Flash bulb	ampoule flash	ampōol fläz̄
Lens	objectif	obs̄ēktif
Movie camera	caméra	kamēra
Negative	négatif	nēgatif
Paper	papiér	papiyē
Glossy	brillant	briyaṉ
Photo, Picture	photo	foto
Photograph	prendre des photos	prēndr dē foto
Print	épreuve	ēprev
Colour print	épreuve couleur	ēprev cōoler
Roll Film	pellicule, rouleau	pēliqul rolo
Shutter	déclancheur	deklanshēr
Take a picture	Prendre une photo	prēndr ēn foto

COLTHING (DIALAGUES)

May I try it on?
Je peux l'essayer?
s̄e pe lēsayē?

I take a size..............
Je fais du.................
s̄e fē du..................

This is...................
C'est....................
sē ....

Too long.
Trop long.
trō loñ.

Too short
Trop court
trō kōōr

Too tight
Trop étroit
trō ētrwä

Too wide
Trop large
trō lärs̄

Can it be attested?
On peut fair des retouches?
on pe fēr dē retōōsh?

.........fits just fine.
.........me va bien.
.........me va biyañ

..........dosen't fit.
.... ne me va pas.
...........ne me va pa.

DRY GOODS

English	French	Pronunciation
Accessories	accessoires	exēsori
Buckle	boucle	bōokle
Button	bouton	bōoton
Elastic	elastique	ēlastik
Hooks and eyes	crochets	kroshē
Lining	doublure	doblur
Needle	Aiguille	ēgei
Sewing needle	aiguille à coudre	ēgei ä kōodr
Pin	epingle	ēpingl
Ribbon	ruban	rubēn
Safety pin	epingle de sureté	ēpingle de syurtē
Scissors	ciseaux	sizo
Silk thread	soie à coudre	swä ä kōodr
Suspenders	bretelles	brētēl
Tape	ruban	rubēn
Measuring tape	centimètre	sentimētr
Thread	fil à coudre	fil ä kōodr
Wool	laine	lēn
Zipper	fermeture	fer mētur

FABRICS

Fabrique:-
fabrik:-

English	French	Pronunciation
Cloth	drap	dräp
Corduroy	velours	velor
Cotton	coton	kotoṉ
Fabric	tissu / étoffe	tisu / ētof
Flannel	flannel	flanēl
Jersey	jersey	zhersy
Linen	toile	twa
Material	tissu / matière	tisu / matiyēr
Nylon	nylon	nilon
Silk	soie	swä
Artificial silk	soie artificiel	swa artifisiyēl
Velvet	velours	velōōr
Wool	laine	lēn
Worsted	laine peignée	lēn pēnē

TOILETRIES

English	French	Pronunciation
After shave	Lotion après rasage	losiyon aprē rasazh
Brush	brosse	brōōs
Clothes brush	brosse à habits	bros ä häbi

Comb	peigne	pēn
Compact	poudrier	pōodriyē
Cream	crème	krēm
Curler	rouleau	rulo
Deodorant	déodorant	dēyodoron
Dye	teinture	tiyantur
Eye liner	crayon à paupières	krayon ä popiyēr
Eye shadow	ombre à paupières	ombr ä popiyēr
Eyebrow pencil	crayon à sourcils	krayon ä sōorsil
Hair brush	brosse cheveaux	bros shevo
Hairpin	épingle cheveaux	ēpingl shevo
Lipstick	rouge à lèvres	rōozh ä lēvr
Mascara	rimmel	rimēl
Mirror	miroir	miruwar
Mouthwah	eau dentrifice	ō dontrifis
Nail File	lime à angles	lim ä ongle
Nail polish	vernis à ongles	vērni ä ongle
Nail polish-remover	dissolvant	disolvon
Perfume	parfum	pärfēm
Powder	poudre	pōodr
Razor	rasoir	rezwar
Razor blades	lame de rasoir	lām de rezwar
Sanitany napkins	serviette-hygiéniques	sērviyēt-hyzhiyēnik
Scissor	ciseaux	sizo
Shampoo	shampooing	shēmpōoing
Shaving brush	blaireau	blēro
Shaving Cream	crème à razer	krēm ä razē
Soap	savon	savon̄

Suntan cream	crème solaire	krēm solēr
Tissues	mouchoirs en papiers	mushwarēn papiyē
Tampoons	tampons	tampoñ
Toiletries	toilette	twa lēt
Toilet paper	papier hygiénique	Papiyē hyzhiyēnik
Tooth brush	brosse à dents	bros ä dēn
Tooth paste	dentifrice	dēntifris
Tooth powder	poudre dentifrice	pōōdr dentifris
Towel	serviette	sērviyet
Bath towel	serviette de bain	sērviyet de bēn

AT THE BEAUTY SHOP

May I make an appointment for Saturday?
Je voudrais un rendez-vous pour samedi?
zhe voodrē ēn rendēvōō pōōr samdi?

For tomorrow?
Pour demain?
pōōr demēn?

Will I have to wait?
Faut-il attendre?
fotil atēndr?

Wash and set please.
Faites-moi un shampooing et une mise en plis.
fēt- muwa ēn shampōōing ē yun mizēn pli.

Please set my hair for the evening.
Faites-moi une coiffure du soir, s'il vous plait.
fēt-muwa yun kwafre duswar, silvōō plē.

Please cut my hair little shorter.
Coupez-moi les cheveaux un peu plus court, s'il vous plait.
kupē-muwa lē shevo enpe plu kōōrt sil vōō plē.

Please pin it up.
Relevez- moi les cheveaux.
rēlevē-muwa lē shevo

Its a little hot under the drier.
Le séchoir est trop chaud.
le sēshwar ē trē sho.

Could you give me a manicure (pedicure).
Pourriez vous me faire la manucure (pédicure).
puriyē - vōō me fēr la manicure (pēdicure).

A facial mask (face massage) please.
Un masque facial (un massage facial), s'il vous plaît.
ēn mask fēsial (un mēsazh fesial) sil vōō plē.

Yes, thank you, that's fine.
Oui merci, c'est bien.
wi, mērsi, sē biyan̄.

AT THE BARBER SHOP

(Shave and) a haircut, please.
Une coupe de cheveaux (et.la barbe), sil vous plait.
yun kōōp de shevo (ē lā barb) sil vōō plē.

Not too short, please.
Pas trop courts, s'il vous plaît.
pa tro kōōr, sil vōō plē.

(Very) short, please.
(Très) court, s'il vous plait.
(tre) ko͞ort, sil vo͞o plē.

At the back.
Derrière.
dēriyer.

On the top.
En haut.
ēn ō.

In front
Devant.
devoñ.

On the sides.
Sur les côtés.
sur lē kote.

A razor cut, please.
Une coupe au rasoir, s'il vous plaît.
yun koop ō razwar sil vo͞o plē.

A shampoo, too please.
Lavez-moi aussi les cheveaux, s'il vous plaît.
levē-muwa osi lē shevo, sil vo͞o plē.

Scalp massage, please.
Un massage, de la tête.
ēn mäsäs̄, de lä tēt.

Would you trim my beard, please.
Taillez-moi la barbe, s'il vous plaît.
taiyē-muwa la barb, sil vo͞o plē.

Just a shave, please.
Rien que la barbe, s'il vous plaît.
riyañ ke la barb, sil vōō plē.

Please leave it dry.
Ne les mouillez pas, s'il vous plaît.
ne lē muiyē pa, sil vōō plē.

Yes, thanks that's great.
Oui, merci, c'est parfait.
wi, mersi, sē parfē.

PHARMACY

Where is the chemist shop?
Où est la pharmacie?
ōō ē la farmasi?

I would like this medicine please.
Ce médicament, s'il vous plaît.
se mēdikamoñ, sil vōō plē.

I'd like..........
Je voudrais..........
že vōō drē..........

Please give me some thing for
Je vous prie de me donner quelque chose contre..........
že vōō pri de me donē kēlkežoz kontr..........

Do I need a prescription for this?
Ce remède est délivré sur ordonnance?
se remēd ē dēlivre sur ordononse?

Can you order this medicine for me?
Pouvez-vous me procurer ce médicament?
poove-voo me prokyurē se mēdikamon?

When can I pick it up?
Je peux l'avoir quand?
ƒe pe lāvoir kon?

Can I wait for it?
Puis-je attendre?
puyi-ƒe ättendr?

AT THE DOCTOR'S CLINIC

Quick, call the doctor!
Appelez d'urgence un médecin, sil vous plaît!
apēlē dyurƒans en mēdsen, sil voo plē!

Is there a doctor?
Y a-t-il un médecin?
Yatil en mēdsen?

Please get a doctor.
Faites venir un médecin, sil vous plaît.
fēt venir en mēdseñ, sil voo plē.

Where is the hospital.
Où est l'hôpital?
oo ē l'hôpital?

Whoud you please come to the..........?
Venez s'il vous plaît au..........?
venē sil voo plē ō..........?

I am sick.
Je suis malade.
s̄e swi maläd.

My husband (my wife, our child) is sick.
Mon mari (ma femme, notre enfant) est malade.
mon märi (ma fēm, notr enfoñ) ē maläd.

I am not feeling well for the past few days.
Depuis quelques jours je ne me sens pas bien.
depyu kēlk zhōōr zhe ne me sēn pa biyañ.

My head (throat, stomach) hurts.
J'ai mal à la tête (au cou, au ventre).
s̄e mal älä tēt (o kōō, o vēntr)

It hurts here.
J'ai mal ici.
s̄e mäl isi.

I have got high fever.
J'ai de la (beaucoup de) fièvre.
s̄e de la (boku de) fiyēvr.

I can't handle the heat here.
Je ne supporte pas la chaleur.
s̄e ne suport pa lä zäler.

I have indigestion.
J'ai une indigestion.
s̄e yun eñdis̄ēstyoñ

I ate.
J'ai mangé.
s̄e mäns̄e.

I threw up.
J'ai vomi.
s̄ē vomi.

I feel sick.
J'ai mal au coeur.
s̄ē mal o ker.

I have no appetite.
Je n'ai pas (d'appétit).
s̄ē nē pa dapetit.

I am constipated.
Je suis constipée.
s̄ē swi konstipē.

I fell.
J'ai fait une chute.
s̄ē fē yun z̄yut.

DINER WITH YOUR FRIENDS

Diné avec vos amis:-
Dinē avek vozami:-

Enjoy your meal!
Bon appétit!
bonäpēti!

Cheers!
Tchin-Tchin!
shin-shin!

Do you like it?
Vous aimez / tu aimes ça?
vōōzēmē sa / tu aim sa?

It is very good. Thank you
Merçi, c'est très bon.
Mērsi, sē tre bon.

That's absolutely delicious.
C'est absolument délicieux.
sē absolumēn delisiye.

Would you like some of this?
Vous en voulez?
vōōzen vōōlē?

This is a French speciality.
C'est une spécialité française.
sētyun spēsiyalitē fransēz.

Would you like some more..........?
Encore un peu de..........?
enkor empde..........?

Yes, please.
Oui volontiers.
wi volontiyē.

No more. Thank you.
Pas pour l'instant, merci.
pa pōōr lēnsta mērsi.

No, thank you. I am full.
Je n'ai plus faim, merci.
s̄e nēpa plyu fēm, mērsi.

What is this?
Qu 'est-ce-que c'est?
kēsksē?

Would you pass me the..........please?
Vous pourriez me passer..........s'il vous plaît?
vōō pōōriyē me pasē..........sil vōō plē?

Do you mind if I smoke?
Ça vous dérange si je fume?
sa vōō dēran̄s si zhe fume?

Thank you for the invitation / inviting me / us.
Merci, pour l'invitation.
mērsi, pōōr lēnvitasiyōn̄.

It was wonderful.
C'était excellent.
sētē ekseleñ.

ON THE PHONE

Au téléphone:-
o telefon:-

Hello! This is..........from..........
Allô! Ici monsieur / madame..........
alo! isi misyu / medäm..........

I would like to talk to..........
Je voudrais parler à..........
zhe voodre parle ā..........

Don't hang up.
Ne quittez pas.
ne kite pa.

..........is on the line right now.
..........est en ligne en ce moment.
..........eton lin en se momō.

..........is not here today.
..........n'est pas là aujourd'hui.
..........nepa lā osordwi.

Would you like to leave a message?
Désirez-vous laisser un message?
dezire-voo lese en mesāzh?

Do you speak French?
Vous parlez français?
voo parle fronse?

Only a little.
Un petit peu seulement.
en peti pe selmeñ.

Please speak a little slower.
Parlez plus lentement, s'il vous plaît.
parlē plyu lontemoñ, sil vōō plē.

Do you understand?
Vous comprenez? / Tu comprends?
vōō komprenē? / Tu komproñ?

I understand.
J'ai compris.
s̄e kompri.

I didn't understand.
Je n'ai pas compris.
s̄e nēpa kompri.

Would you please repeat that?
Vous pourriez répéter, s'il vous plaît?
vōō pōōriyē rēpētē, sil vōō plē?

What is this called in French?
Comment ça s'appelle en français?
komo sa sapēl en fronsē?

What does..........mean?
Que signifie..........?
ke sinifi..........?

READING AND WRITING

Lire et ecrir:-
lir ē ēkrir:-

I would like..........
Je voudrais............
še vōōdrē..........

An American / English newspaper.
Un journal américain / anglais.
en šōōrnäl āmērikēn / onglē.

An American / English magazine.
En magazine américain / anglais.
en māgzēn āmerikēn / onglē.

A map of the area.
Une carte de la région.
yun kart de la rēšiyoñ.

Do you have more current issue?
Vous aurriez aussi un journal plus récent?
vōōzoriyē osi en šōōrnäl plyu rēsen?

AT THE TOBACCONIST'S

Au taba:-
o tābā:-

A pack of filtered / unfiltered cigarettes please.
Un paquet de cigarettes avec / sans filteres s'il vous plaît.
en pākē de sigārēt avek / son filter sil vōō plē.

A carton / pack of..........please.
Une cartouche / un paquet de..........s'il vous plaît.
yun kartoosh / en pākē de..........sil vōō plē.

A pack of pipe / cigarette tobacco, please.
Un paquet de tabac pour la pipe / à cigarettes s'il vous plaît.
en pākē de täbä pōōr la pip / ä sigärēt sil vōō plē.

Could I have a box of matches / a lighter please?
Une boîte d'allumettes / un briquet s'il vous plaît?
yun bwāt dālumēt / en brikēt sil vōō plē.

LEGAL HOLIDAYS

All saints day.
La toussaint.
la tōōsēn.

Christmas.
Noël.
noyēl.

Christmas eve.
La veille de noël.
lā vēy de noyēl.

Easter.
Pâques.
päk.

Mardi gras.
Le carnaval.
le kärnäväl

New year.
Le jour de l'an.
le soor de lēn.

New year's eve.
La saint-sylvestre.
lä sēn-silvēstr.

THE DATE

La date:-
lä dät:-

What's the date today?
Quelle est la date aujourd hui?
kēlē lā dāt ozhordwi?

Today, it is July 2nd.
Aujourd'hui c'est le deux juillet.
ozhordwi sē le de juiyē.

On the 4th of this month / of next month.
La quatre de ce mois / du mois prochain.
le katr de se muwä / du muwä proshēn.

Until March 10th.
Jusqu'au dix mars.
zhusko di mars.

We are leaving on April 15th.
Nous partons le quinze Avril.
nōō pärtoñ le kēnz Āvril.

We arrived on November 16th.
Nous sommes arrivés le seize Novembre.
nōōsom zarivē le sēz novombr.

THE WEATHER

Le temps:-
le tōmp:-

What's the weather going to be like today?
Quel temps va-t-il faire aujourd'hui?
kēl tom vātil fēr ozhordwi?

Have you heard the weather forecast?
Vous avez déja écouté la météo?
vōōzavē dēzha ēkōōtē lä mētiyo?

It is going to be / get..........
Il fait / va faire..........
il fē / va fēr..........

Warm	chaud	sho
Hot	très chaud	tre sho
Cold	froid	frwä
Cool	frais	fre
Humid	lourd	loor

It is windy.
Il fait du vent.
il fē du vēn.

It is very windy.
Il y a dela tempête.
il yä delä tompēt.

What is the temperature?
Quelle est la température?
kēlē la tompērätur?

It looks like rain / a storm.
On dirait qu'il va pleuvoir / faire de l'orage.
on dirē kil va pluvwar / fēr de lorazh.

POLICE: LOST AND FOUND

Where is the nearest police station?
Où est la poste de police?
o͞o ē la post de police?

Does anyone here speak English?
Est-ce-qu'il ya quelqu'un qui parle anglais?
ēskilya kēlkēn ki parl onglē?

I would like to report a theft.
Je voudrais déposer une plainte pour vol.
ʒe vo͞odrē dēpozē yun plēnt po͞or vol.

I would like to report an accident.
Je voudris faire une déclaration d'accident.
ʒe vo͞odrē fēr yun dēklorasiyon daksidont.

My daughter / son has disappeared.
Ma fille / mon fils a disparu.
ma fi / mon fis a dispäru.

My..........has been stolen.
On m'a volé..........
on mä volē..........

My car has been broken into.
On a ouvert ma voiture par effraction.
onä o͞ovēr ma vuwatur pär ēfraksiyon.

I need a copy of the official report for insurance purposes.
J'ai besion d'une attestation pour mon assurance.
s̄e bēswän dyun ätēstäsiyoñ po͞or mon äsuronse.

I would like to speak to my lawyer.
Je voudrais parler à mon avocat.
s̄e vo͞odrē parlē ā mon avoka.

I am innocent.
Je suis innocent.
s̄e swi inoson.

ABBREVIATIONS

A.C.F French Automobile Association.
Automobile Club de France.
otomobil klub de Frons

A.J. Youth hostel
Auberge de Jeunesse.
obērs̄ de s̄enēs.

B.P. Post-office box.
Boîte postale.
bwät pastäl

C.C.P. Postal cheque account.
Compte de chèques postaux.
kompt de shēk posto.

C.U. University camp.
Cité Universitaire.
sitē univērsitēr.

dép Departure.
départ.
dēpar.

m Mister.
Monsieur.
misyu.

mlle Miss.
Mademoiselle.
medmwäzēl.

mm	Messieurs. Messieurs. mēsiyer.
mme	Mistress. Madame. madäm.
O.R.T.F.	French Broadcasting Corporation. Office de la Radiotélévision française. ofis de la Rädiyotēlēviziyoñ fronsēz.
P. et T.	Post and Telecommunication. Postes et Télécommunications. postē tēlēkomunikäsiyon.
pl.	Square. Place. pläs.
R.F.R.	System of suburban express train. Réseau express régional. rēzo exprēs rēzhionäl.
R.N.	Federal Highway. Route Nationale. rōōt nasiyonal.
S.A.M.U.	Life-saving-service. Service d'aide médicale d'urgence. sērvis dēd mēdikal durzhons.

S.N.C.F.	French Railroad. Société Nationale des chemins de fer Français. sosiyētē nasiyonāl dē shemeñ de fēr fransē.
S.I.	Tourist office. Syndicat d'initiative. sēndika denisiyativ.

SIGNS

To let.
À LOUER.
ä luyē.

For sale.
À VENDRE.
ä vēndr.

Stop.
ARRÊT
ärē

Arrival.
ARRIVÉE
ärivē.

Attention / Caution.
ATTENTION.
ätonsiyoṉ.

Public notices.
AVIS AU PUBLIC.
ävi o publik.

Second floor.
DEUXIÈME ÉTAGE.
deziyēm ētäs̄.

Entrance.
ENTRÉE.
ontrē.

No Admittance.
ENTRÉE INTERDITE.
ontrē enterdit.

Entrance Free.
ENTRÉE LIBRE.
ontrē libr.

Escalator.
ESCALIER ROULANT.
ēskaliyē rulon.

Fire Extinguisher.
EXTINCTEUR.
ekstinkter.

Do not open.
NE PAS OUVRIR.
ne pa o͞ovrir.

Refreshments.
BUVETTE (BAR).
buvēt (Bar)

Ladies.
DAMES.
däm.

Danger.
DANGER.
donzhēr.

Mortal danger.
DANGER DE MORT.
donzhē de mor.

Paste no bills.
DÉFENSE D'AFFICHER.
dēfons däfishē.

No smoking.
DÉFENSE DE FUMER.
Dēfons de fumē.

No swimming allowed.
DEFENSE DE SE BAIGNER
dēfons de se bēinē.

Also Available

Quick and Easy *Way to* Learn HINDI

PT. ADITYA NAND

Rs. 130/-